PSYCHOSOCIAL PRACTICE
WITHIN
A RESIDENTIAL SETTING

THE CASSEL HOSPITAL MONOGRAPH SERIES

Series Editors

Peter Griffiths and Pam Pringle

THE CASSEL HOSPITAL MONOGRAPH SERIES

PSYCHOSOCIAL PRACTICE WITHIN A RESIDENTIAL SETTING

Edited by

Peter Griffiths and Pam Pringle

Caroline Flynn *Peter Griffiths*
R. D. Hinshelwood *Fritha Irwin*
Roger Kennedy *Graham McCaffrey*

Foreword to the Series by
R. D. Hinshelwood

London
KARNAC BOOKS

First published in 1997 by
H. Karnac (Books) Ltd.
58 Gloucester Road
London SW7 4QY

British Library Cataloguing in Publication Data

A C.I.P. record for this book is available from the British Library.

ISBN 1 85575 177 7

Edited, designed, and produced by Communication Crafts

Printed in Great Britain by BPC Wheatons Ltd, Exeter

10 9 8 7 6 5 4 3 2 1

ACKNOWLEDGEMENTS

The following have been adapted and reproduced by permission:

Chapter 2, from R. Kennedy, "Work of the Day". In R. Kennedy et al., *The Family as In-Patient*. London: Free Association Books, 1987.

Chapter 3, from C. Flynn, "The Patients Pantry: The Nature of the Nursing Task". *Therapeutic Communities*, 14 (4), 227–236.

Chapter 4, from G. McCaffery, "The Use of Leisure Activities in Psychosocial Nursing". In E. Barnes et al., *Face to Face with Distress: The Professional Use of Self in Psychosocial Care*. London: Butterworth Heinemann, 1997.

Chapter 5, from F. Irwin, "The Therapeutic Ingredients of Baking a Cake". *Therapeutic Communities*, 16 (4), 263–268.

CONTENTS

FOREWORD TO THE SERIES

R. D. Hinshelwood

This is the first in a series of monographs intended to present accessible teaching texts concerned with the practice of residential care. Residential care is beset not only by inherent difficulties, but also by notorious scandals. There is a reason for this. Residential care demands that people are at close quarters with harrowing and disturbing human agonies and predicaments. Often those difficulties are without immediate prospect of being relieved, or the outcome of care is only a very limited achievement.

The work is therefore perhaps one of the noblest of careers.

However, all—residents and staff—are exposed on a long-term basis to these stresses, which take their toll in terms of personal morale and integrity. As a result, it is not surprising that in certain circumstances strange and alarming behaviour results.

Unfortunately, residential care is often provided by young, inexperienced, and insufficiently trained people. This may be because carers soon give up the stress and move on to other things; or, because, with seniority, people move themselves quickly away from the pressure of "coal-face" work.

How can those who choose this career be better supported and their personal resources enhanced to withstand better the emotional impact of the stress? It is a fundamental principle behind this Series that a professional stance can be learned and, indeed, taught. We would contend that the most effective support for practitioners is to be clear about the way they work, and to think in terms of a model that they carry in their minds of what residential care consists of.

Too often, inexperienced new recruits arrive with their own—sometimes exaggerated—expectations of what they aim to do and the way in which they expect to do it. And, too often, the expectations of each member in a team of staff are in conflict, contradicting each other and not worked out with each other at all. Such a situation throws a heavy burden on the leadership to get a coherence out of a rag-tag team.

In consequence, this Series offers as clearly as possible a specific model of care, which has grown up over half a century at the Cassel Hospital. It is a highly professional model. And, possibly uniquely, it also protects the personal involvement of the staff within the network of human relationships within the care organization. In other words, it is based not simply on procedures to be carried out, but also on the emotional reactions aroused when carrying them out. Its message is that the human feelings of the staff can be used professionally—and they are thus stopped from being an impetus to other, strange, disordered or unethical responses.

We make no claim that the Cassel method of psychosocial care is the only model for residential work, though there is perhaps not a very large selection of alternatives. The method is, however, well worked out, and a very great deal of experience has accumulated. The resilience to stress of each person in a trained team of staff is strengthened through the use of a single model of professional care. In turn, the members of the team support and strengthen each other through a stronger sense of working together.

The purpose of these monographs is to present this model of care on a wide basis, and to complement the development of the professional courses in psychosocial practice that are currently run by the Cassel Hospital or are in process of development. Subsequent monographs in this Series will focus on other aspects of this practice—patients, staff, institutional factors, and so forth. An important development of this model will be in translating it from its original setting—in a hospital for people with severe personality disorders—to organizations caring for other kinds of people, and in other, and non-residential, settings.

R. D. Hinshelwood
September 1997

INTRODUCTION

Peter Griffiths and Pam Pringle

The closure of mental hospitals taking place on a national scale has led to a rise in the numbers of smaller community-based units for people with mental health problems. Residential units now provide the settings for a variety of professional practitioners. Different and new skills are needed in order to care for, and work alongside, clients.

Since the foundation of the Cassel Hospital after the First World War, a method of using the residential environment as a means for therapeutic change and transformation has evolved in this specialized setting. The patients treated at the hospital today comprise individuals (adults and adolescents) and whole families who have severe emotional and social difficulties. Many patients have long psychiatric histories, involving self-mutilation, suicide attempts, and over-use of psychotropic medication. Traumatic family backgrounds of separation, loss, deprivation, and physical, emotional, and/or sexual abuse are also often a feature of our patients' lives.

Patients come into treatment carrying the marks of these traumatic histories and present-day problems, but they also come to us with the hope for development and change. Whole families are admitted together, with the possibility of being reunited, and are allowed the opportunity to learn how to provide a more stable and nurturing environment in which children can grow and flourish.

Our aim is to enable our patients to realize their emotional and social capacities. In simple terms, we believe that this model of residential treatment can help people to begin to care for themselves and others.

Treatment consists of various components, but the most important of these are individual psychotherapy, psychosocial nursing in the context of the therapeutic community, and patients working together within the framework of hospital life (Griffiths & Leach, 1997).

Although our patients frequently have severe borderline or schizoid personality disorders, we believe that psychosocial practice has much to offer to those working with clients in other areas of mental health care, social services, education, and the criminal justice agencies. Psychosocial practice attempts to create an environment that turns experience into learning. It is a practice that utilizes both the daily domestic and recreational aspects of living and the interchange between clients/patients and staff working (and possibly living) together as a focus of enquiry and a medium for treatment.

In the first of the chapters here, Peter Griffiths and R. D. Hinshelwood discuss the rationale for the development of a culture within hospitals and residential institutions that wish to concern themselves with mental health (as opposed to mental illness), and in which patients or clients are enabled to take on an active role in their treatment. They describe the evolution of such a culture and the practice of psychosocial nursing at the Cassel Hospital, a practice that encourages patients to use everyday tasks and relationships as a means both of managing their disturbance and for exploring the possibilities for transformation and growth. The importance of giving patients real responsibility is emphasized; however, the authors also point out the need for understanding the feelings that this can generate in such patients. Helping patients to tolerate the feelings of responsibility and guilt through words, but especially through actions, forms an essential part of psychosocial care.

Roger Kennedy puts forward the idea of "the work of the day" as a medium for therapeutic work. He suggests that the everyday events in the ordinary course of the day—events that we normally take for granted, such as sleeping, washing, cooking, eating, and working—provide both a basic framework for living, but also structures for thoughts, feelings, emotions, and intimacy with others. For individuals and families with psychological and emotional disturbance, these structures have usually broken down, yet they hold special significance for these individuals and families. They precipitate thoughts, feelings, and actions that provide the material and therapeutic potential for both psychotherapy and psychosocial nursing work. Clinical examples are given to illustrate this concept.

The subsequent chapters illustrate the way in which everyday activities can be seen as having, for individuals, both internal/intrapsychic and external/interpersonal conditions of existence and how these can be used to therapeutic effect.

Caroline Flynn concentrates on a particular aspect of the nursing work and thus offers an introduction to the essence of psychosocial practice. She uses the example of the "Patients' Pantry" to show how a domestic activity—managing the hospital's food supply—can provide a rich medium in which therapeutic work can take place.

Social and recreational activities also form part of the therapeutic programme. Graham McCaffrey describes how these are integrated into the psychosocial nursing work. He gives examples of the therapeutic opportunities that emerge when nurses and patients work together on managing and participating in leisure activities. He also discusses some of the difficulties in mixing "work" and "leisure" for both patients and staff.

In her chapter, Fritha Irwin describes the therapeutic gains made by a patient whilst managing the social activity of "cake making" alongside the nurse. The patient has also contributed a short evaluation of her experience.

These chapters together describe how the residential environment at the Cassel and the domestic and recreational activities that form a framework for everyday living are in themselves valued and used as a means for therapeutic change. However, it is the people operating within that framework—the patients and the staff—who act as agents of change and transformation.

Attention is drawn to the nature of the role of psychosocial nurses and their practice. The role itself is a complex one, which nurses have an opportunity to sample through training as part of the Diploma in Psychosocial Nursing and in their employment on the different hospital units. However, the practice of psychosocial care need not be confined to one specialist hospital. The capacity for reflection and action and the ability to engage in the life and events of a community of individuals is a feature of many institutions. What we hope to show through these illustrations of working life at the Cassel is the creative use that—through sensitivity and skill—may be made of ordinary events. The generation of an understanding of the past and present experience for the patient can be coupled with an awareness of his or her own talents and abilities, as well as present limitations. Functioning capacities can be discovered and enhanced, and disturbance can be more readily worked with. The outcome can be one of hope and development for the patient.

The work is not easy. As Griffiths and Hinshelwood discuss, staff can be subject to unconscious processes and defence mechanisms that mitigate against the development of a "healthy institution". The regressive pull towards an omnipotent state of mind, whereby staff have all of the answers and patients none of the solutions, is a consistent difficulty. In order to deal with the dilemma of working to provide care but also share responsibility for the outcome of treatment, nurses require support and supervision. We stress the need for opportunities to enquire into professional practice and to manage the often disturbing feelings that working closely with our patients brings. This is a fundamental area and one that will be further explored in a subsequent monograph in the series, on sustaining a culture of enquiry.

Psychosocial practice comes at a price. Involvement in our patients' lives, working alongside them and sharing their hopes, fears, problems, and joys, can be difficult and demanding. It means an enquiry into our motives for practising our professional skills and a questioning of our abilities. However, the rewards can be professional and personal development for ourselves and therapeutic change and transformation for our patients.

ABOUT THE AUTHORS

Caroline Flynn, SRN, RMN, Diploma in Health Studies, Cassel Cert, worked at the Cassel Hospital for ten and a half years before leaving in the spring of 1994. She is currently Senior Nurse Advisor, Riverside Mental Health Trust.

Peter Griffiths, Bsc, SRN, RMN, Cassel Cert, is a lecturer in Psychosocial Practice at the Cassel Hospital and has a particular interest in developing psychosocial practice in other health care settings through consultancy, courses, and training. He is a visiting lecturer at the Tavistock Clinic and a member of the editorial board of the journal *Therapeutic Communities*. He is a co-editor of *Face to Face with Distress: The Professional Use of Self in Psychosocial Care* (Butterworth Heinemann).

R. D. Hinshelwood is Clinical Director of the Cassel Hospital. He is a Member of the British Psycho-Analytical Society. He founded the *International Journal of Therapeutic Communities* and the *British Journal of Psychotherapy* and is author of *What Happens in Groups*, *A Dictionary of Kleinian Thought*, and *Clinical Klein* (Free Association

Books) and of *Therapy or Coercion: Does Psychotherapy Differ from Brainwashing?* (Karnac Books).

Fritha Irwin, SRN, SCM, Cassel Cert, was a clinical nurse specialist for the therapeutic community team at the Cassel Hospital, where she worked for seven years, and was involved in teaching and training both within and outside the Hospital. She recently contributed a chapter for E. Barnes et al., *Face to Face with Distress* (Butterworth Heinemann). She is now in full-time education, undertaking an MSc.

Graham McCaffrey, BA, RGN, Cassel Cert, worked at the Cassel Hospital for six years. He worked on the community team and was senior nurse on both single adult and families units. He is now living in Calgary, Canada.

Roger Kennedy has been a Consultant Psychotherapist to the Families Unit at the Cassel Hospital since 1982. He trained in Child Psychiatry at the Tavistock Centre and Guys Hospital and is a Training Analyst with the British Psychoanalytical Society. He co-authored *An introduction to the Work of Jacques Lacan* and *The Family as In-patient* and is author of *Freedom to Relate* and *Child Abuse, Psychotherapy and the Law* (Free Association Books).

Pamela Pringle, MSc Interprofessional Health and Welfare Studies, BA(Hons), RGN, RMN, Cassel Cert, is currently an Outreach/ Research Nurse at the Cassel Hospital. She is researching through clinical practice the development, elaboration, and use of a model of psychosocial practice in the community.

PSYCHOSOCIAL PRACTICE
WITHIN
A RESIDENTIAL SETTING

CHAPTER ONE

Actions speak louder than words

Peter Griffiths and R. D. Hinshelwood

People in hospitals, whether working as staff or there as patients, experience the hospital in both conscious and unconscious terms. The thesis of this chapter is that we need to enquire about the unconscious "hospital in the mind" that staff and patients carry with them. We enquire first about the ways in which this intrapsychic object informs their thoughts, behaviour, actions, and feelings, as this object becomes externalized through the roles they take up and the relationships they form. Emphasis is placed on the possibility for both the treatment and the treatment setting to rob an individual of his or her functioning capacities and on the importance of enabling patients and clients to take on an active role in their treatment. We then explore the practice of psychosocial nursing at the Cassel Hospital, which encourages patients to use everyday tasks and relationships both for containing their disturbance and for exploring the potential for change and transformation in their lives.

As our starting point, we consider some of the ideas and thinking that went into the development of the Cassel Hospital as a psychoanalytically orientated therapeutic community after the

Second World War. At this time, Tom Main (1946) wrote of traditional hospitals:

> The concept of the hospital as a refuge too often means, however, that patients are robbed of their status as responsible human beings. Too often they are called "good" or "bad" according only to the degree of their passivity in the face of the hospital demand for their obedience, dependency and gratitude. The fine traditional mixture of charity and discipline they receive is a practised technique for removing their initiative as adult beings, and making them "patients". They are less trouble thus to the staff. Hospitals that follow this orthodoxy are usually designed for the individual treatment of the individual patient by an individual doctor, not in a real social setting, but in a state of retirement from society. . . . Within such a setting, health and stability are often bought at the excessive price of desocialisation. Sooner or later the patient, alone and unsupported, must face the difficult task of returning to the society in which he became unstable, and there again regain social integration and a daily sense of values and purpose. This task is no light one for a desocialised man, however *healthy* [italics added] he may have become.

He further suggests:

> The design of the hospital as a social retreat also ignores positive therapeutic forces—the social support and emotional opportunities that are granted in spontaneously structured communities. . . .
>
> Treatment of the neurotic patient, who suffers from a disturbance of social relationships, cannot therefore be regarded as satisfactory unless it is undertaken within a framework of social reality that can provide him with opportunities for attaining fuller social insight and for expressing and modifying his emotional drives according to the demands of real life. [Main, 1946, pp. 7–8]

In both of these quotations Main suggests that hospitals may actually harm patients by rendering them unable to cope in ordinary society so that even if mentally recovered, they have succumbed to a social disability instilled by the hospital. A little later, Barton (1959) and Goffman (1961), among others, made similar and more detailed observations, based on their research and studies, of the iatrogenic effects of institutions on their occupants. However, Main also attempted to identify the complex intrapsychic, interpersonal, and psychodynamic processes at play, suggesting that, in such situations, staff and patients tend to become creations of each other:

> In most hospitals the staff are there to care for others less able than themselves, whilst the patients hope to find others *more* able than themselves. The helpful and the helpless meet and put pressures on each other to act not only in realistic but also in fantastic collusion and in fantastic hierarchical systems. The actively projectively helpful will unconsciously *require* others to be helpless, while the helpless will *require* others to be helpful. Staff and patients are thus inevitably to some extent creatures of each other. [1975, p. 12]

In short, as carers we are all driven to find helpless people or people in need, an impulsion derived by our own conscious and unconscious needs. Main suggests:

> We know that doctors and nurses undertake the work of alleviating suffering because of deep personal reasons and that the practice of medicine, like every human activity has abiding unconscious determinants. [1957, p. 33]

Roberts (1994) suggests more forcefully that in choosing to work in a helping profession,

> The choices we make regarding which profession to train for, which client group we work with and in what kind of setting, are all profoundly influenced by our need to come to terms with unresolved issues from our past. [p. 110]

Patients, simply by virtue of being patients, are driven to find magically helpful others to restore them to health from death and madness.

This collusive dance is to some extent mitigated by the realities of work, and the difficulties are very much in conscious awareness. However, with disturbed people in psychiatric or mental health work, the pressure of these unconscious dynamics and phantasies is very much greater. In psychiatric work, the hospital needs to check this as much as it is able. It cannot do so at all unless there is a proper awareness of the unconscious, and a proper respect for its power over us. It would be wrong to assume that this dynamic is limited to residential institutions; it can also be found in the contemporary culture of community mental health care, where there are perhaps fewer checks, or no means for the exploration of such psychosocial dynamic forces. In this setting, they also need to be recognized and worked with if they are not to have a disabling effect on patients, clients, and staff alike.

Main believed that the first treatment priority should be the prevention or correction of the potential dynamic iatrogenic effects of treatment that the patient is required to carry. He suggested the therapeutic community technique as a useful check on institutional collusive projection—and its accompanying dangers to the personality of *all* concerned (Main, 1983). Together with the nurses at the Cassel, he sought to institute within the hospital a culture that prevented the desocialization and removal of adult responsibility. He and they began a long process (see Main, 1957; Weddell, 1968) to develop a healthy institutional culture, one that recognized the dependency needs of patients and staff but equally checked their regressive excesses—a culture that would not only protect the patients, but would also provide an actively enhancing role within the treatment. He later suggested:

> A therapeutic community is one of on-going enquiry about personal and group anxieties and defences and of endeavour to create adaptive, thought-out roles, relations, structure and culture geared to reality tasks and relevant to the capacities and needs of the individuals within the community. This is in contrast to the classical medical organisation model in which only roles of health or illness are on offer; staff to be only healthy, knowledgeable, kind, powerful and active, and patients to be only ill, suffering, ignorant, passive, obedient and grateful. [Main, 1957, p. 103]

In brief, the development of the treatment milieu at the Cassel has been described by Griffiths and Leach (1997) as comprising three interrelated aspects:

1. individual psycho-analytic psychotherapy; in conjunction with this,
2. psychosocial nursing practice which takes place in the context of the therapeutic community; and

3. patients working actively with each other in the ordinary life of the community. [Griffiths & Leach, 1997, p. 2]

In the remainder of this chapter we explore further and reflect upon the unique form of psychosocial practice that has developed within the nursing service (i.e. point 2 above—sychosocial nursing), a practice that, to some degree, patients emulate as auxiliaries in the nursing of each other.

The Cassel model of psychosocial nursing

Flynn suggests in Chapter 3 that the psychosocial nurse's role: "is wide and encompasses many aspects that do not fit into the more traditional ideas of what nurses are 'supposed to do'. Likewise patients' roles within the institution deviate from what is normally expected" (p. 38).

The role is to interact and "be with" patients in an everyday way. The role of the nurse *is not* occupational therapy, *it is not* to occupy the patient in between treatments, *nor is it* to care for patients in need of care. The nurse may, nevertheless, play some part in all of these things, in conjunction with other nurses and—as importantly—with other patients.

The hospital's residential living and working environment forms the basis for the therapeutic milieu and the framework within which nurses undertake their work with patients. The hospital has the capacity to admit up to 61 patients. There are three units: Adult, Adolescent, and Families. Patients are admitted for anything between six and eighteen months (families tend to stay longer than individuals). Patients live at the hospital during the week but are generally expected to go home at weekends. All are admitted with severe emotional and social difficulties.

An emphasis is placed on patients establishing a living environment that encompasses as many everyday activities as possible; there is a further emphasis on the patients as managers of these activities. Activities may be the household ones of cooking, cleaning, gardening, maintenance, and child-care; or they may be leisure activities such as badminton, singing, cake baking, or holidaying;

or they may be activities of care of each other when in crisis or distress, when new, or when leaving. Many, or most, of these activities involve groups, and patients must therefore be managers of a group. Patients are thus required to care for themselves, for each other, and for the community.

It is believed that real responsibilities (and accountabilities) offer opportunities for both success and failure. The creation of a safe supportive environment, in which patients can experience failure and disappointment, as well as success, is an important part of the work with patients in that it offers reparative possibilities. The development of pride in positive capacities and successes helps patients to cope with the inevitable pain in accruing insights into troubled areas of their personality; such development is also the point of the psychological work in both their psychotherapy and in their work with patients and nurses. Within the psychosocial milieu there is an emphasis on three particular aspects: responsibility, reparation, and self-esteem.

Inevitably, disturbed patients at times fail at these responsibilities (and indeed success can be equally alarming). Moreover, usually they are initially affronted at being expected to engage in something so different, or even alien, from their expectations of unconditional care by doctors and nurses. The extensive introduction of each patient to the community through a series of assessment meetings often does little to diminish these powerful, idealized expectations and unrealistic wishes borne out of previous treatment and unconscious needs (Denford & Griffiths, 1993). This is deeply stressful for patients, for not only are their expectations so deeply confronted, but when they do try to cooperate with such an unexpected system, they often find themselves hard-pressed to succeed at anything. Faced by this stress, it is impressive how much their preceding symptomatology by which they expressed themselves fades away, to be substituted by a hostile vocal (or silent) protest at the hospital and the staff. In such a protest they often find the beginnings of real colleagueship, though that can hardly be the endpoint.

The role of the nurse at the Cassel Hospital is radically different. It is not to "run the place", but to support patients in the stress of being community members and in carrying out and undertaking the personal and interpersonal expectations that the hospital expects of them, from personal functions such as sleeping at night, going to bed at a reasonable hour, washing, wearing clean clothes, and eating meals at the allotted times with others to more interpersonal functions such as domestic cleaning, cooking, child care, caring for others, receiving care, engaging in social activities—functions that many of our patients have previously been unable to manage at home, whether alone or with others.

Irwin suggests in Chapter 5 that

> An important part of the philosophy of our work at the Cassel Hospital is to maintain the expectation that patients can function as responsible adults despite their often evident disturbance. . . . The activity managers are expected to be reliable and responsible about organizing their activity. They may at times feel distressed and want to "collapse"; our culture in the hospital would encourage them not to regress and give up but to obtain support from others in order to continue with everyday life. [pp. 65–66]

The psychosocial nursing role is one of support and encouragement—of "working alongside" the patients, as it is put. Patients who have often broken under the weight of responsibility will not be expected to put the burden down, but to seek and find the necessary support to carry on—support from each other to share the burden, and support from the nurses in finding others to share it with them. This is not to deny the distress, disability, and disturbance that these patients experience, which can be quite common in caring institutions (Miller & Gwynne, 1972). We merely mean that, through support, patients are encouraged to explore alternative ways of managing their disturbance and, through developing and using everyday relationships, gain effective support.

The crux of the matter is that psychosocial practice offers tasks with *real* rather than contrived responsibility, as only that way can patients experience real success or failure. And that is what real everyday life is about.

The nurses' role in psychosocial practice is arduous because it confounds their *own* earlier, and latterly professionally, internalized expectations of what they should be doing—providing succour, care, and relief for suffering human comrades. It is also arduous because those they seek to help in this way are, for long periods, uncertain about their wish for this unexpected kind of care. It is believed that human dependency on others evolves over the lifespan, taking different forms, and is not simply an undesirable regressive state, to be combated and ultimately eradicated by health care professionals. The need for some dependency in patients is recognized, and this may vary over time. Time of increased dependency need not equate with lessened responsibilities, and the relationship between the two is by no means inverse. The ability to take responsibility may itself need to be learnt or relearnt. Nurses strive to work towards a sharing of responsibility for care and the outcome of treatment with patients.

This complex and by no means straightforward process forms the basis of the nurse–patient relationship. Similarities and differences between the respective roles of nurse and patient are not denied but acknowledged, and they form the basis for a potential collaborative alliance for work with the patient. This alliance also allows for the inevitable conflict that arises because of differing responsibilities, roles, expectations, and levels of mutual identification and understanding.

Very great emphasis is therefore placed on the support and supervision of nursing staff. Nurses can hold on to hope and hopefulness only if they can own and contain their own omnipotent phantasies of absolute cure and its converse: total impotence or failure (Dartington, 1994; Meinrath & Roberts, 1982). The potential for change can be realized more fully if the nurse believes in the existence and value of a psychosocial dimension to care, rather than seeing the provision of care as a one-to-one curative act determined by the performance of a particular skill or intervention and performed by the "active nurse" upon the "passive patient" (Main, 1957). An individual's best hope for change may instead be located within and held singly—or in a combination of the physical, psychological, or social domains—at an individual, interpersonal, group, or community level of action and intervention. Only supported and contained staff can provide the interpersonal medium required to achieve therapeutic change and transformation in patients.

The role of working alongside

Crucial to this practice is the relative weight given to verbal inter-change (the medium of psychotherapy and psychoanalysis) and actions (the medium of psychosocial practice). This is clearly brought out by Gillian Chapman, who remarks that if "a patient is to be viewed as an independent adult [that] means he must also be held responsible for his own actions" (Chapman, 1984, p. 70). She goes on to say:

> Furthermore, the patient should experience in a realistic way the consequences of these actions. Should he break, lose or destroy a piece of the community's equipment, like an iron, the nurse is required to follow through, with the patient and doctor, the consequences of this action. This would involve developing an understanding of the meaning of the act to the patient and sharing it with other patients and staff. Under-standing would be followed by deciding with the community whether the patient should repair or replace the equipment, or whatever might be the appropriate way to facilitate repara-tive actions. Such events can evoke strong feelings and conflicts between the people concerned. [p. 70]

Thus:

> Talk is only one aspect of the nurse's role. Nurses participate in the community at the same time as observing it. Nurses act in the community both through talk and by working along-side patients in the practice of day-to-day living. [p. 71]

We emphasize here, and indeed throughout this text, (1) the importance of the community's *work of the day* as the focus of psychosocial practice, (2) the importance of *real* responsibility, and (3) above all that the process and output of psychosocial practice is activity of one kind or another *alongside* patients.

What is specific to this form of practice is that at its core is a cycle: actions (and accompanying thoughts and feelings) give rise to actions, with understanding as an intermediary. Action and activity can be used defensively to fend off thoughts and feelings, but within psychosocial practice the crucial and unique aspect is the intermediary step—understanding, which here is derived from actions (and thoughts and feelings about these) and is later expressed in further actions.

Responsibility

The particular place of responsibility is addressed over and over again in psychosocial practice, and it is the single most potent distorting influence in the actions that make up the living-together environment of the community. It has therefore the most central place in the intermediary step.

The intermediary step is one of enquiry, thought, and understanding, and there are no doubt many conceptual frameworks that will supply sufficient purchase on the problem of understanding odd or dangerous action. However, such conceptual frameworks need, in this instance, to revolve around the nature and psychodynamics of responsibility and the many means that people employ to avoid responsibility or its consequences.

Living together demands a willingness and ability to feel responsibility for each other. Simple activity in the Patients' Pantry team, for instance, is given its relevance and realistic quality because the needs of colleagues in the community may suffer or be met, depending on the performance of the patient. If he or she "forgets" to get the meat out in time to defrost, then the community will be in for a meagre supper. In such an instance, the patient becomes responsible both for his or her action (or lack of it) and its accompanying feeling and for the feelings that this may stimulate in others. These latter feelings of others maybe related to the immediacy of the event and the patient, or may resonate with earlier experiences of deprivation and lack of nurture.

Responses to such a position of responsibility are legion amongst disturbed people, and understanding such responses requires considerable sensitivity on the part of the nurse and the rest of the community. At the Cassel, the most frequently used means of understanding derives from the concepts of psychoanalysis. Nurses and patients (through example) use their own transference and countertransference feelings, both in an immediate and often active way, and in a more thoughtful, reflective way, in the responses and interventions they make in such a situation.

Let us dwell for a moment on the way that responsibility can be thought about, in general, within a psychoanalytic framework. Responsibility weighs heavily on the superego, which can provoke (or merely threaten) quantities of guilt. Unconscious guilt or the fear of it is central to a great deal of mature and civilized living. Undue guilt has a harshness that is intensely persecuting and torturing and leads to swift and often inventive means for evading it, typically through various slick means of avoiding the responsibility from which it arose. Patients afflicted in this way, with a problem with their superego, therefore need intense support to carry the responsibilities that can lead to crushing guilt. Other patients may be so internally overwhelmed that they give up evasion, and in fact give up activity of all kinds in a debilitated, crushed state. Still others may respond to the invitation to take responsibility in a paranoid way, as if it were an actual external persecutor rather than an internal self-torture. Many other distorting and maladaptive devices may be used to gain relief from this kind of burden—all the way to the mind-blowing condition of the schizophrenic (see, for instance, Segal, 1956).

It is now understood that there is a more useful path by which the feelings of responsibility and guilt may be psychologically tolerated. This involves methods of making repair, often to substitute objects (as McCaffrey suggests in Chapter 4). In one of the quotes above from Chapman, a broken iron might, realistically, be mended if the patient gains sufficient support—though hardly without some sparks flying!

The point is that guilt has to be tolerated long enough, even unconsciously, for the person to make amends. In the longer term, experiences of making satisfactory reparation usually ameliorate the strength and harshness of the superego and the guilt that emanates from it. In addition, the task of making physical amends requires the use (and or development) of a degree of ego strength, as the person is required to bear a degree of uncertainty as to its outcome and to contain the intrapsychic and real separating out and reintegration of the parts of the task. In the first instance, such ego strength needs support from both nurses and patient colleagues.

It is clear that supporting someone to make physical amends is a form of practice—no amount of talking about the transgressions (real or otherwise) can do as much as practical acts of reparation.

Action, reflection, meaning, and practice

We have presented a form of practice that takes the form of a set of cycles, moving from actions, to reflection and understanding, and then back to actions—a form of psychodynamically informed action learning.

Each of these three steps may involve the use of words in various ways to carry information, to keep relationships going, and to assist in the provision of support. However, it is the actions that count therapeutically and developmentally. Gabbard (1992), in discussing psychoanalytically informed treatment, suggests that the non-interpretative aspects of therapeutic action may be mutative in their own right, and that actions and inter-actions contain interpretative messages. He importantly notes that, with seriously disturbed patients, such as those seen in hospital settings, the notion of providing a holding environment constitutes in itself a form of interpretation-in-action. Actions carry meaning, and these meanings can be discovered and expressed in a medium that is not verbal but is the medium of psychosocial practice—action on and with bodies.

> For example, a woman who was diagnosed with chronic schizophrenia relapsed when she was sent to a home in the community (Hinshelwood, 1987). When readmitted to the rehabilitation ward, the key worker (a nurse) was puzzled by the woman's bizarre psychotic symptoms and also troubled that some were tactile hallucinations located in the patient's vagina. After a long investigation process it was eventually noted that the patient had been transferred to a home where there was a notorious male exhibitionist who flagrantly exposed himself without restraint on any occasion. From then it was simple to realize that back in the rehab block she was now accommodated on a floor where all the other rooms were taken by men.

The lack of awareness in the staff team, until time for reflection was offered, was matched by the incomprehensibility of the psychotic symptoms. Once meaning could be discerned in the patients sexual symptoms and their cause, it was then possible to take meaningful action, and reorganize the room allocation in the rehab block. That action, the reorganization, serves to carry meaning for the patient in the form of action much more effectively than any verbal discussion or interpretation of her symptoms.

Though words are the prime vehicles of meaning in adult culture, this is not so in babies, who are dependent on the mother/carer's understanding and learn from that maternal understanding to understand themselves. A baby's development is through a communication process with the mother that is entirely non- and pre-verbal. Psychotic patients often use words less like symbols and more like the concrete vehicles of meaning that resemble actions. In other words schizophrenic patients operate at the level of a "language of action", and an action such as reorganizing the room allocation conveys understanding and the potential for self-understanding very much more than does verbal interpretation. Of course, much can go wrong with a language of action—just as with a language of words. But it is as if people at first, as babies, need to master a language of action before moving on to a language of words (and in the process forget much of the language of action that they needed as infants), yet in the development that is therapy the priority of actions may also apply (Ogden, 1991, p. 365)

To have thoughts and then to think originates in the experience of feeding. The development of thought has a great deal to do with the mother–baby relationship. At the beginning of the relationship, the mother has simply to try to feel and understand what the baby wants and needs. As the mother develops a knowledge of the baby's needs using her own feelings to guide her, she is able to differentiate between hungry, discomforting, and desperate cries. With the satisfaction of mothering and the attunement the mother conveys, the baby learns to wait and take on the capacity to contain and understand his own anxieties himself, through introjection (Grunberg, 1979).

Psychosocial nursing—and possibly all nurturing activity involved with the provision of physical safety and of physical and psychological care—perhaps stimulates an awareness of this early non-verbal language through action. However, it is a language that may originally have been absent or distorted for many of the patients with whom we engage. Psychosocial practice makes use of this resonant connection, through the creation of a specialized environment for treatment: consistency in timetable and reliable social structures, in conjunction with real expectations of the patient in a reality-orientated, yet safe holding environment (Winnicott, 1960). Non-verbal understanding—achieved through the registering of symbolic action, actions, and their contingent, non-action—provides both intrapsychic containment and the opportunity for a transformational reparative experience, for both the child and the adult in the patient. Through the process of psychosocial practice, nurses mediate the connections between earlier experience and present-day experience and promote the possibility for change and growth.

Conclusions

The processes that result in the creation of division between staff and patients, which we described at the beginning of this chapter, come straight out of a psychodynamic and psychoanalytic way of understanding unconscious processes and defence mechanisms. In particular, what we described was the projection—by the staff into the patients—of attributes of helplessness, passivity, ignorance, and so on. Patients then introject the staffs' projections and act up to their character. At the same time, patients project their adult functioning selves, health, wisdom, responsibility, and so forth into the staff, who happily accept them through introjection and act up to these more powerful attributes (Conran, 1984). Dependency and irresponsibility in patients, often described as symptoms, often have more to do with collusive participation in the hospital/care system. The processes of projection and introjection as described by psychoanalysts are very common and very visible in groups and organizations.

Or they would be visible—if our own insight were not clouded by being ourselves caught up in these processes. When they work under the peer pressures of an institution, psychoanalysts and psychotherapists are equally caught up, just like anybody else. We need, all of us, to be on our guard, yet this does not mean that we all have to *be* psychoanalysts or psychotherapists.

One of the ways in which psychiatric nursing is developing is for nurses to become counsellors within the wards, community centres, or community psychiatric nurse teams (Peplau, 1952, 1994; Winship, 1995). We would agree that there is a need for this. However, what we have attempted to share with you here is a different path for psychiatric nursing and mental health workers to tread—that of psychosocial practice—which, in our view, is equally necessary.

Tom Main's point is that an individual treatment of an individual patient by an individual therapist can rob a patient of his status as a responsible human being. We emphasize again that the potential for change can be more fully realized if the nurse believes in the existence and value of a psychosocial dimension to care, rather than seeing the provision of care as a one-to-one curative act determined by the performance of a particular skill or intervention, performed by the "active nurse" upon the "passive patient". An individual's best hope for change may instead be located within a combination of interventions in the physical, psychological, or social domain, at individual, interpersonal, group, or community levels of action.

This leads to a very important point. Being a counsellor in a hospital or residential setting is not the same thing as counselling outpatients. We need to think therapeutically about the psychodynamics of being a counsellor, as well as the dynamics of doing therapeutic counselling. We need to reflect on the effect of actually being a counsellor and on the transference to the counselling, as well as to the counsellor. There are two different levels: one, at the level of the individual person, where we can use our knowledge to do good counselling; and another that is different, at the level of the social institution, where we can employ our knowledge both to understand how being in counselling can itself make the patient *less* responsible and also to understand the disabling rifts that may develop between the patient and the nurse or worker. We should do what we can to avoid robbing a patient of his status as a responsible human being—whatever the counselling, psychotherapy, pharmacotherapy, or other individual attention, a truly therapeutic milieu must take into account this potential for robbery.

We have not been talking about nurse counselling, but about psychosocial nursing practice, with the distinctions that we have elaborated.

With the advent of care in the community, there has been a proliferation of small units of mental health workers providing mental health care within residential and non-residential settings. Whilst there are a variety of different practice and management models in operation, the two are rarely linked into one coherent model. Moreover, there is an absence of any theoretically integrated clinical model that underpins both practice and clinical management. This results in a provision of care and treatment which is often individualized (and provided by a range of individuals), inconsistent, fragmented, and often frustrating as much for patients as for staff. The therapeutic potential of the environmental context, the social interpersonal milieu, and the person is rarely realized, leading to a sense of failure.

The Cassel Hospital has pioneered an action-based integration of psychoanalysis and social systems theory, resulting in a particular model of psychosocial care and treatment which works with the psychological and social aspects of the individual. It is a model that views the person as a holistic, multidimensional system: physical and psychological states of being are interwoven at interpersonal, familial, group, and social levels of being. Each person contains a mixture of functioning and non-functioning and (perhaps unhealthy) parts, strengths, and weaknesses—both internally and in relationship to others—in his or her psychosocial environment. Health and ill health are not absolute states but are defined through an interaction between internally and externally derived factors. Human development is a lifelong holistic process, components of which may stay constant, stagnate, regress, or evolve over time. The potential for change and transformation may, as mentioned above, be located in a variety of psychological and social domains.

The psychosocial model we have elaborated involves an inter-related understanding and practice in these various domains and, in particular, in the use of actions and activity, as well as words, phantasies, and the real social representations that express them in the therapeutic work. Psychosocial practice attempts to create an environment that turns experience into learning. It is a practice that utilizes both the daily domestic and recreational aspects of living and the interchange between patients and staff working (and possibly living) together, as a focus of enquiry and medium for treatment.

CHAPTER TWO

Working with the work of the day: the use of everyday activities as agents for treatment, change, and transformation

Roger Kennedy

This chapter owes a deep debt to the work of Dr Tom Main during his years at the Cassel Hospital. One of his achievements was to transform a model of in-patient treatment of mental disturbance in which regressed patients were being attended to and passively nursed, into one in which the patient is actively involved in the psychotherapy and nursing processes. I put forward here the simple idea that central to this new model is the notion of what I call the ordinary work of the day, around which is focused both psychotherapy and the psychosocial nursing work. I am limiting the concept of the work of the day so that it does not refer merely to everything that happens in the day, but only to those events that are significant in some way to the individual and his or her family or have precipitated some kind of thought process and/or action. Thus, the work of the day would include unsolved problems, major worries, overwhelming experiences, undigested thoughts, forbidden or unresolved thoughts, what has been rejected and suppressed, and what has been set in motion in the unconscious by the activity of the preconscious and consciousness. It refers to all the significant, and at times deceptively indifferent, thoughts, feelings, and experiences that have occupied us during the day and provide the raw material for thinking and for dreaming. The work of the day is what gives material for thought and provides the basic framework of living.

Much of this work normally carries on automatically without us being particularly aware of its regular occurrence or of its "everydayness", and without our giving much attention to it. The work is normally taken for granted, and yet it is far from simple in nature, as you can see from the treatment of disturbed families and individuals where such basic work has broken down. The work of the day is normally focused around essential activities and events such as eating, sleeping, and working. Such events, ritualized and structured to a varied extent, provide the emotional context that drives practical life. Our reliance on everyday structures and rituals, however sophisticated, to hold us together may have something to do with the nature of our emotional life, in which feelings are often fleeting; we seem to need something solid and relatively unchanging to help us pin our feelings down in order that we may acknowledge or study them. It would appear, then, that a major task of the work of the day is, as it were, to enable us to "discover" our emotions through ordinary everyday events and tasks. Such events, even though they may seem trivial, form common human intercourse and provide the basis for intimacy. Indeed, one could say that true intimacy between people often consists of being with each other in ordinary, everyday situations without feeling awkward.

Normally one performs the activities of the day without thinking about their basic structure; rather, the basic structure provides material for thinking. However, in the patients I am discussing, the things most people do without thinking—such as sleeping, washing, eating, eating meals with others, as well as more interpersonal functions such as cooking, cleaning, caring for others, receiving care, and being involved in social activities—are charged with emotion and conflict, to the degree that there is a breakdown in the continuity and consistency of daily life. The life of the day is not "held together". One could describe this in Winnicott's terms as a breakdown in the individual or family's "holding" environment (Winnicott, 1960).

There are some similarities between what I have called the work of the day and the place and function that Freud ascribed to the day's residues and waking thoughts in the formation and interpretation of dreams. Freud emphasized the importance of recent events and the relevance of waking thoughts in the instigation of dreams. The significance of recent events and fresh impressions has not had time to be lost through the processes of repression. The instigating agent of a dream is found among the experiences that the subject has not yet "slept on"; that is, these are often undigested experiences. Freud described how the material that has occupied us during the day dominates the dream, and how one can understand dreams as a continuation of waking life. Displacement and the use of indirect representation are mainly responsible for the dream's puzzling appearance, which disguises this continuity. Freud wrote (1900a, p. 177) that the "analysis of dreams will regularly reveal its true psychically significant source in waking life, though the emphasis has been displaced from the recollection of that source onto that of an indifferent one". Freud also wrote that the day's residues (1911b, p. 273) "have the most numerous and varied meanings; they may be wishes or fears that have not been disposed of, or intentions, reflections, warnings, attempts at adaptation to current tasks, and so on". The day's residues are thus the psychical material for the dreamwork to act upon.

The unconscious wish is the essential additional factor in the construction of the dream. This wish can come to expression in the day's residues and can supply them with a force that enables them to press their way to consciousness. Particular unconscious conflicts can be, as it were, "hooked" or "transferred" onto the recent material, and the latter can provide a point of attachment for such conflicts. Similarly, returning to the theme of the chapter, one could say that the unconscious weaves its connections around the work of the day. In psychoanalytic treatment, one may be looking for past conflicts through the processes of reconstruction and interpretation of the transference, and yet one hopes very much that one is working with fresh material from recent events—that is, from the work of the day—as such material has not yet been bogged down by the processes of repression and is often rich in content. Indeed, one could go so far as to say that, as long as the present and the ordinary events of a patient's life are in the treatment, one can more easily uncover the repressions of the past. As Freud demonstrated in *The Psychopathology of Everyday Life* (1901b), one is often led from the commonplace to the physically significant. However, I am also emphasizing the psychical significance of ordinary events, not only as a point of attachment for unconscious conflicts, but in their own right as the framework for living.

The breakdown of the work of the day

The Cassel Hospital provides a unique opportunity for looking at the day-to-day, week-to-week living arrangements of adolescents, adults, and whole families. I concentrate here on our work with families, as this is the area with which I am most familiar.

The families we treat are in general in an extreme state of breakdown and are often barely able to cope with the ordinary tasks of living together. One often also notices that they have begun to drain the resources and patience of involved professionals in the world outside the hospital. There is often, for example, the threat or reality of a care order to one or more members of the family, or the threat that a member of the family will leave home. During our assessment procedures we try, among other things, to look at how families bring their own pathology and "living space" into the hospital—that is, how they bring in the pieces of their reality and repeat their breakdown within the hospital. This breakdown, both in an individual and in his or her family, can be seen as a piece of inner reality that has not stood up to social reality, where there has been a conflict between the family and their milieu. This is invariably repeated on admission to the hospital in one way or another; however, it takes different families a different span of time for this repetition to occur. The repetition seems to have a time course of its own.

There are many factors leading to family breakdown. These include individual factors such as an important member of the family who is strained or who may have an individual breakdown or illness. There may, on the other hand, be group factors in the family; that is, the family may not function effectively as a group. There may be chance events or important life events; there may also be developmental factors—for example, the challenge to the family's functioning that is made by the maturing of an adolescent child. One often finds in such families that the work of the day has broken down in the outside world and that ordinary tasks are not given enough attention. When this occurs, the family or particular vulnerable members of the family may well be subjected to over-whelming anxieties. The work of the day may break down when there has been severe social stress or when there has been what I call "malignant splitting" in the family—that is, a repeated and intense use of primitive splitting mechanisms in the family's object relations, common to most of the families we happen to treat, which interferes in a major way with the family's capacity to at-tend to normal functions, or a breakdown of the normal social barriers—for example, when there has been sexual abuse by one member of the family of one or more other members.

Although we see a wide range of both individual and family psychopathology, one can, in general, see a breakdown in the process of working over or metabolizing thoughts and feelings from hour to hour, from day to day, and from week to week. That is, there is a breakdown in the day's structure that provides both the material and the space for thinking and enables the subject to discover his or her feelings. Normal events are then experienced as persecutory and lacking in continuity; thinking about them seems painful and useless. The physical and psychic "bricks and mortar" of the family home become loose and fragmentary, and the capa-city to keep partners and children in mind becomes eroded. An increasingly wide gap appears between the parents' knowledge of their family life and their capacities to use this knowledge. Some families reach a point where they seem hardly able to attend to events such as organizing mealtimes or bedtimes; in addition, they often resort to impulsive actions as a way of trying to get the environment to respond to their needs.

As is well known, one often finds that one or more parents of such families have suffered from fairly severe emotional or physi-cal deprivation in childhood. In more theoretical terms, one could speculate that there has been an absence of the primary infantile experience of satisfaction, what Freud called the "bedrock of psychic life" (1900a, p. 602). These parents seem to have experienced a repetitious absence of satisfaction in their childhood, as a result of parental or social deprivation. As adults, they often try to seek some satisfaction, but in unsatisfactory ways. For example, many deprived patients feel desperately needy and have a hope or a fantasy that the damage done to them can be totally made up. This may lead to a desperate search for resources—for example, from professional workers—but the patients will never feel that what they get is good enough. They thus tend to drain the patience and capacities of those who try to help them, and so they end up repeating the absence of satisfaction that they were apparently so desperately seeking to avoid. It is noteworthy in this context that we often find a family, on admission to the hospital, to be in severe financial debt, with a related housing crisis.

In the members of the families that I am describing, who to all intents and purposes have never had much basic experience of satisfaction, rational thinking has in Freud's terms never come to "safeguard" the primary processes (Freud, 1913a). With the families we treat, there is often a fantasy present that thinking interferes with their life and is both persecutory and unhelpful. Putting the situation simply, the patients avoid the possibility of acknowledging their distress and of allowing themselves to have thoughts. In addition, there may be a pattern of turning to an inner, precarious fantasy object or attempting to make an external object fit in with the inner fantasy object; there may be also sometimes a turning to "alternative resources" such as drugs or perverse sexual excitement. What such patients do to children, relatives, friends, or carers can also be seen as an aggressive attack on their own internal parents. This latter attack may be contained in their symptoms. For example, when real parents neglect their real children, this may represent an attack on the internal parents. This could also be seen as turning a passive childish experience into an active adult one. We often see this in those adult patients in the hospital who apparently want constant parenting, or appear very needy, and yet, in spite of considerable efforts by staff and other patients, avoid effectively using hospital structures or any kind of out-patient psychotherapy. Instead, they constantly and desperately bite the hand that feeds them; at the same time, they seem unaware of the aggres-

sive aspect of their demands. Such patients are well described by
Tom Main in his classic paper, "The Ailment" (Main, 1957).

Another major theme, central in trying to understand the origin of the breakdown of the work of the day, is how the parents in
these families often feel that they cannot take on their role as parents, at least for a whole day. This may occur for a variety of
reasons, such as a lack of their own parenting, their immaturity,
the envy they may feel towards their children, or social pressures.
One could in general say that the birth and presence of a child are
highly complex and powerful for the adult. A child may awaken
past conflicts and re-open old narcissistic wounds; the adult may
be quite capable of inter-adult relations, but quite incapable of
responding to the child. One often sees in families in the hospital
how difficult it may be for some parents, on the one hand, to keep
their adult capacities and ability to respond to their children separate and intact, and, on the other, to satisfy their own childlike
dependency needs. In extreme situations, the child's presence may
precipitate such a disruption in mental functioning that the child
will be subjected to primitive and unmodified psychic or, indeed,
physical attacks at the hands of the adults, who can no longer
distinguish the child from the unwanted bad parts of themselves.
The child may also become the object that unites or divides a
family; the child will then be, as it were, a "child object" for the
family, a mere function and not a person. One might also speculate
that the breakdown in the parents' parenting and in their ability to
attend to the basic everyday events around the child's day is
linked to an earlier breakdown in their own experience of being
parented, either at adolescence or perhaps at the period of primary
parental preoccupation, when their parents had to keep them actively in the front of their mind for much of the day, but did not.
There would often seem to be the repetition of a basic gap in the
parents' thinking as it concerns the child.

The work we do at the Cassel Hospital with families involves
a unification of psychoanalytic psychotherapy and psychosocial
nursing practice. In general the hospital pays particular and focal
attention to the work of the day in the total treatment of individuals and families. It becomes the focus for the detailed work of
analysing sources of disability and distress. In particular, we look
at what happens during the day at events such as eating, feeding

of babies, night-time preparation tasks such as cleaning, and structured meetings. The achievements and conflicts from day to day and from week to week around these events become a central focus of attention. Neuroses, like dreams, have a tendency to belittle the importance of the details of working life and relegate them to a realm of indifference. As Freud wrote (1911b, p. 218) "every neurosis has as its result the forcing of the patient out of real life". However, the Cassel Hospital focuses on these details: all the penumbra of resistances, denials, associations, and material that occupies the hospital during the day becomes a main agent of treatment and, hopefully, of change, and it is hoped that such material provides the focus, or at very least the background, for both the individual psychotherapy and the detailed and intensive psychosocial nursing work. Severe splitting mechanisms, common to many of the patients we treat, have a tendency to obscure individual emotions and conflicts. For this reason, we put particular emphasis on the details of what has happened to particular individuals and what they have experienced, and on the work that the nurse and therapist of a particular patient are doing. We explore the nature of the nurse–therapist relationship, as this often reveals much about the pattern of the relationships the patient is developing to either; the origin of these often having a basis in their (the patients') earlier experience (see James, 1986). We emphasize the individuality of the patient's feelings and provide a framework for individualized thinking.

At the same time, there are a number of different group activities in the hospital. We can see that the group has certain useful functions: for example, it may serve as a mediator of projections, as well as the unique source of information of unconscious processes. In general, through individual and small-group supervision, staff meetings, and, in particular, the supervision of the relationship between the nurse and therapist of particular patients, we aim to provide a setting in which the patient can reflect on himself or herself and for the registration and understanding of distorted communications and distorted relations. Yet, as Alan Wilson has put it, "the psychotherapeutic community is not a stable, polite society: it is a prescription of uncertainty . . . free association, but free association observed with focal attention" (Wilson, 1986, p. 63). The hospital does not provide rigid rules, nor, on the other hand, does it believe in free-for-all, unbounded chaos. It aims to provide daily structures in which uncertainty and indeterminateness can be tolerated and worked with. In particular, in our treatment of families we aim to work with and support the parents' "authority". This refers to the parents' capacity to allow and tolerate a child to be dependent on them and to appreciate the child's world, with its need for good-enough security, flexibility, warmth, and understanding on a day-to-day, hour-to-hour basis. It is our experience that there are a number of disturbed families who need in-patient treatment because such basic daily work has broken down in the outside world, making them no longer viable as a unit. Our major aim is often to enable such families to recover or discover their capacities to deal with the "bricks and mortar" of their physical and psychic home. To a greater or lesser extent, such therapeutic work may be more important to these families, at least at the time of their admission, than more traditional understanding of the psychopathology of the individual members, although this work also usually continues during admission.

Clinical examples

I first attempt to show, through two examples, how essential activities in the families' functioning can break down. I then demonstrate, through a further two examples, how such externalized breakdown affects the functioning of the hospital but equally how such a disturbance in function can, if it is detected and processed, be put to therapeutic use.

Example 1
FAMILY A: FEEDING TIME

This family was admitted as an emergency following a domiciliary visit. The problem was that the mother was suffering from a severe postnatal depression after the birth of her second girl baby. Mrs A was depressed and distraught and said that she felt unable to stay in her own home. Although the birth was satisfactory, Mrs A said that she had problems feeding the baby. The baby refused to take anything from the bottle and would cry as if in anger. The mother described this supposed failure at feeding as the trigger of her problems, and she started to feel anxious, panicky, inadequate, and tearful, with increasing intensity, until her admission when the baby was 5 months old. "I feel so guilty", said Mrs A: "I'm not giving her what she wants, I'm not special to her; after all, anyone can give her a bottle."

The crisis point was reached when Mrs A lost control and shut herself in the bedroom screaming, not able to deal with the baby's crying. She felt she was on a knife edge: she was afraid of losing control and afraid of slipping into madness, but at the same time she felt it would be nice to regress to a childlike state and to be looked after. Mrs A was able to respond quite well to both her children, but only separately. There were major problems at feeding time, when she seemed unable to cope with the two children together. In addition, the 2-year-old would rush around at meals, trying to get her mother's attention; indeed, when Mrs A was feeding the baby, the older child used to writhe around on the floor, screaming. Mr A in general felt inadequate and unable to support his wife in the way she felt would be helpful. This made him feel angry, but he was unable to express this anger.

Most of Mrs A's anxieties were increased at feeding times. These anxieties included a feeling of wanting to run away, thoughts of disappearing in a puff of smoke, and suicidal preoccupations. She felt trapped when the baby wouldn't feed; the baby's demands made her feel inadequate and overwhelmed. While disappointed at giving up breast feeding after two months, she was also concerned at her own weight loss. In therapy sessions, she at first disclosed how closely she identified with the baby: she said how very much she wished to become like a little girl herself and admitted that she wanted to be held, cuddled, fed, and looked after.

The first area of attention in treatment was the mother–child relationship, with particular emphasis on feeding, as so many of the family's problems seemed to arise at this time or at any rate to be increased in intensity. It is interesting that, as treatment proceeded, Mrs A revealed her own "feeding" difficulties: a predominant feature of the family's early admission was the feeling of deadness that they provoked and evoked in other people. There was a massive denial of feelings of attachment to the hospital and to each other. Anything we offered the family was not accepted as good enough; Mrs A arranged for a special kind of vegetarian meal for herself and managed to have her meals before the other patients, which seemed to be indicative of her increasing social isolation in the hospital. She then revealed in detail a number of sadistic fantasies she had in relation to the baby. The family became outsiders in the Families Unit; they were unpopular and would not accept our help as of any use. They constantly maintained the idea of discharging themselves in a month's time, an idea that they held to, in fact, for a number of months.

Staff on the Unit found that they were being intimidated by Mrs A's threats to leave and exploited by her demands to be given very special treatment. While staff were disagreeing with each other, the family itself seemed to be doing very little in the hospital. However, when this was realized by the staff and then raised with the family, the treatment began to move. There was considerable work done on the theme of mourning, on difficulties in the couple's relationship, as well as on work with the children. When a staff member produced the concept of presenting the family with a "staying date" rather than a leaving date, the treatment turned the corner. The family settled down to detailed work, and there seemed at last to be a reasonable "feeding" relationship between the family and the hospital; the family was considerably improved on discharge and at the six-month follow-up.

Example 2
FAMILY B: CONNECTING AND PLAYING TOGETHER

Mrs B, a woman in her early 20s, and her son James, aged 5 years, were referred in order to attempt to bring them together after a number of separations. Mrs B had been hospitalized following an overdose and had shown great difficulty in coping with her son. Indeed, he had been put into care twice and was being fostered prior to admission.

Mrs B showed evidence of severe psychopathology with marked schizoid features, together with a tendency to lapse into primary-process thinking and action. For example, following her consultation, she shaved her head completely bald and wandered about looking like a baby. Mrs B came from a large family of mixed race; her father was described as very strict; he used physical punishment to discipline the family, who were expected to be at his beck and call. Her mother was described as sacrificing her life for her children; she still behaved as if they were all babies. Mrs B was intelligent and had done well at a good school, but she married aged 18; this interrupted her education. Her husband walked out when she became pregnant, and he did not take part in their subsequent life. James was a bright child but was difficult to manage because of his behaviour difficulties; in particular, he had a large vocabulary of abusive language, which he often used.

An important dynamic in the mother–son relationship seemed to be a faulty connection. This was illustrated not only by their difficulties in staying together before admission, and Mrs B's inability to attend to James' needs, but also from problems after birth, when there was a difficulty in breast-feeding. The story was that Mrs B was told that her nipples were not long enough; she attributed the great difficulty that she had in trying to feed James to this. She described how somehow James could never take the breast and, later on, how he was not interested in taking food from her.

In psychotherapy sessions in the hospital with Mrs B, there was also great difficulty in the "connecting up" of the therapist and Mrs B. There were long silences; the therapist had a countertransference feeling that she was being shown what it felt like not to be in touch with what was going on in Mrs B's inner world. Mrs B often spoke in disjointed, unfinished sentences, especially when describing her angry feelings with

James, and she often talked as if she and the child were merged as one. She described the feeling that because she had James she must not talk about herself; however, she also realized that this was perpetuating her own mother's view of the world.

Initially, Mrs B was somewhat isolated in the hospital; she somehow missed being included in the community rota for washing up, breakfast duty, and cooking. However, she worked efficiently in her work area, which was the children's playroom and at children's teas, but it was difficult to share a task with her and she gave people the feeling that she was just going through the motions. Her nurse felt that he had to do all the work in making contact with Mrs B; she brought nothing to him. James settled down to some extent in the Day Unit (hospital school), but he could only be managed on a one-to-one setting; his abusive swearing irritated both the staff and other children. As admission proceeded, Mrs B found a useful niche for herself in community cooking, and she seemed to derive a genuine sense of personal validity from this role. Her sullen withdrawal from people and her resentful "going through the motions" was challenged over the issue of how she managed children's teatime. In addition, a major piece of work, which facilitated Mrs B and James "connecting up", was done when her therapist and nurse met both Mrs B and James for regular play sessions for a few weeks. Mrs B's capacity to play with James was encouraged, and some limited interpretation of symbolic material was made. Individual psychotherapy was subsequently arranged for James.

There were many improvements in the relationship between Mrs B and James. Attention to both the psychodynamic meaning of the resentment about being a mother and a capable adult, and attention to the basic work of being a mother during the day, seemed fundamental to the changes that took place; this enabled both of them to live together once more on a more stable footing.

Example 3
FAMILY BREAKDOWN IN THE CONTEXT OF THE HOSPITAL

It was early September, just after the summer break. In the weekly whole-hospital staff group meeting, the following themes arose.

It had recently been discovered that various consulting-rooms had been broken into, which was quite an unusual occurrence at the hospital. There was talk of doors being left open and rooms being emptied or feeling empty. There was a query about whether or not confidential material had been seen. There was a feeling that this was one example of intrusions into private areas which were, perhaps, taking place in other areas of the hospital, outside the consulting-rooms. There had been one or two major staff changes recently; people were feeling that boundaries between members of staff were shifting and new boundaries being made. In addition, there had been a recent increase of night-time disturbances, in which the duty nurse had been put under considerable stress and had to do more work than is customary in order to help patients settle for the night.

In the staff group, a specific family, whom I shall call the "C" family, then became the focus of discussion. The family consisted of a mother, father, and baby aged 9 months; they had been admitted as an emergency following a domiciliary visit, as the mother was in a severe state of postnatal depression and could no longer look after the baby.

They had a rather horrific history in that their first child was born severely brain-damaged, probably as a result of a severe antenatal haemorrhage. Although the doctors looking after this first child felt that it should be allowed to die as it was so severely damaged, Mr and Mrs C managed to keep the baby alive for some eight months by means of intensive nursing care, in which they would take turns virtually 24 hours a day to keep it alive. The baby died when, needing a rest, Mr and Mrs C gave it back to the hospital to care for, for a week or so. Just at this time, Mrs C conceived the new baby. She subsequently had great difficulty in attaching herself to it and could hardly differentiate the dead baby from her live baby. In addition, there was a violent marital relationship with constant rows, as well as severe obsessional near-psychotic psychopathology in Mrs C.

Following the general themes in the staff group, it was then discovered that the C family had become special patients. It was recognized that they did not attend any of the daily work groups in which all patients participate with nurses to look after areas of the hospital. For many weeks they had not been going home on weekends, so that there had been absolutely no differentiation of boundaries between the week and the weekend. This was also most unusual, as it is an expectation that families go home for the weekend in order to maintain contact with their outside world, unless there is a very special reason for them not to be doing so. The family were not on a community cooking rota; other patients had become fed up with doing everything for them, and in addition there were quite marked differences of opinion between the nurse and therapist of Mrs C, resulting in the therapist realizing that she should take up much more of the patient's hostility towards her in the transference.

It was realized that by coupling the general themes of the group with this particular family, there was something to be learnt about the family's psychopathology and how the hospital staff were (or perhaps were not) dealing with it. The empty rooms in the hospital seemed to be related to the empty space in Mrs C in which there was no new baby. Mr and Mrs C wished for special intensive care with no boundaries, with no return home at the weekend. They also wished to remain in their own private world, which was against the expectations of living in a community. They felt that sharing their private world was an intrusion into their rigidly held private space, rather than a chance to be able to share anxieties.

After this meeting, the staff from the Families Unit was able to take up much more vigorously what the family had been doing and what they had been avoiding until then.

Example 4
GENERAL THEMES

For my last example, I have chosen to give a number of typical general themes that arise in the Families Unit and become the focus of attention.

Towards the end of one particular week, approaching the Christmas holidays, it had been noted by the hospital administrator as well as by some of the nursing staff that a number of cigarette ends had been found around the hospital. The place was beginning to look quite untidy, and there was doubt about whether these cigarette ends had been left by the patients, by the staff, or by the group of electricians who were in the process of rewiring the hospital. The rewiring work had entailed knocking a number of large holes, probably at times rather unnecessarily, into the plaster, so that the place was beginning to look a mess. There was a general feeling that the fabric of the hospital had been interfered with in a damaging way. Members of staff as well as patients had mixed feelings about what was happening: some people felt that this was the price one had to pay for modernization, others that the whole job had been botched.

In general, in the patient group and in various meetings throughout the hospital, there was a fear of latent madness getting out of hand and a wish for the staff to take over responsibility. In addition, there was quite an angry, defiant independence; for example, many patients were not returning in time for their Sunday supper. This resulted in the children making it difficult for the parents to put them to bed on Sunday night, and they also became quite disruptive in the Monday morning playgroup. The parents' wish to be looked after seemed to become greater than their wish to be adults and parents for their children. There were general, rather typical, complaints that there were not enough staff or that the nurses were not available, and that staff had too high expectations of what patients were able to do.

However, it was generally felt by staff that a number of patients were at this moment avoiding issues in their own treatment. It was also discovered that there was an interference in the way that the milk was being supplied; a number of bottles of milk had gone missing. Suddenly, the Families Unit found itself without enough milk. It turned out that individuals were plundering the milk without letting anybody know. In addition, one mother (Mrs B in Example 2) had been taking off the cream from the milk and had been feeling quite guilty that no one had discovered this until that week.

These various themes and observations are of course complex, and one cannot very easily link all the themes to particular individuals. However, the fact that the fabric of the hospital had been interfered with, as well as the fact that there was a coming break, obviously precipitated feelings of rage, helplessness, and a wish to be looked after on the part of the patients as a whole. Such feelings in the hospital are interpreted to some extent on a group level and, more generally, on an individual therapy basis, while the expectation is maintained that whatever parents' feelings are about wanting to be looked after, they are still expected to maintain their authority as parents to their children. Any other attitude on the part of the staff would really be a perversion of their work and an inappropriate use of their resources. Mrs B's own particular plundering of the cream of the resources in terms of the cream from the milk was taken up quite vigorously in her individual therapy sessions.

Conclusion

The Cassel Hospital creates and provides a structure in which attention can be paid to those everyday activities that most people take for granted—activities that have both intrapsychic and external conditions of existence in which past experience, present-day expectation, and external reality meet and around which psychotherapy and psychosocial nursing can be focused.

Events such as eating, cooking, feeding babies, cleaning, and playing—the work of the day—can become a means of analysing the origins of the breakdown for disturbed families and individuals. They also enable our patients to recover and discover their functioning capacities. Everyday activities are often charged with emotion and conflict for these patients, but they provide the material that becomes one of the main agents of treatment and hopefully of change and transformation.

CHAPTER THREE

The Patients' Pantry:
the nature of psychosocial practice

Caroline Flynn

T he purpose of this chapter is to convey the value of using the working relationship as a therapeutic tool in working with individuals who have had disrupted and unhappy experiences in relationships with others. Psychosocial nursing practice at the Cassel is highlighted and, in particular, the work of patients and nurses within the "Patients' Pantry" workgroup. In the context of this therapeutic setting, the Patients' Pantry is considered symbolically in terms of a "potential space", as described by Winnicott (1970)—a space in which individuals have the opportunity to demonstrate their creativity within a circumscribed, relatively reliable system. Examples of work with three patients demonstrate how the clinical problems and difficulties encountered can be thrown into relief, so that they become difficult to deny and thereby more available to the process of introspection and hence open to the possibility of transformation and growth.

Psychosocial nursing at the Cassel Hospital

The nurse's role at the Cassel Hospital is wide and encompasses many aspects that do not fit into the more traditional ideas of what nurses are "supposed to do". Likewise, patients' roles within the institution deviate from what is normally expected. Together, nurses and patients undertake many everyday tasks, including cooking, eating, cleaning, decorating, gardening, shopping, playing games, running playgroups, and looking after children.

It may not require a highly qualified nurse to do the washing-up alongside a patient. Yet in carrying out practical tasks, it is desirable for a nurse to have accurate knowledge about, say, what temperature water needs to be to kill certain pathogens or why it is essential, for example, that a certain food is stored for only 48 hours. Such practical and common-sense advice is more convincing if the nurse understands the rationale for such guidelines and can speak with some authority. However, it does require a skilled and sensitive nurse, with a high degree of empathy and a sound knowledge of people's inner workings, if tasks such as washing-up are to be used therapeutically to gain access to the emotional life of the patient. Nurses need to be aware of the background history of the individual patient and to understand how neglect, abuse, or other traumata may affect their ability to relate to other people, and how they tend to feel or respond to current situations, including the work situation. A skill in helping people to talk and listen to one another may facilitate within people the feeling of being heard and listened to by the nurse but also, more importantly, by the peer group or members of the patient's own family.

The nurse also needs to know something of the patients' physical health in order to try to help them understand that the way they feel emotionally may be related to their physical status and vice versa. The nurse, especially, needs to be able to help patients to help themselves in order to deal with physical manifestations of their emotional states.

Knowledge and understanding of the above and a firm theoretical training (Griffiths & Leach, 1997), coupled with a sensitive understanding of personality development and therapeutic change, form the basis of the core skills that are required in order to practise psychosocial nursing effectively at the Cassel Hospital.

In addition, nurses need to have emotional maturity, tenacity, and a belief in the unquenchability of human beings' capacity to grow, learn, change, and develop, in order to live their lives creatively. Put another way, nurses require the capacity to be able to hang on to hope for, and about, their patients, in order to withstand the sometimes relentless emotional attacks to which severely emotionally damaged neurotic individuals subject professional workers. It is important that nurses are able to hold this hope for and on behalf of their patients, especially at times when patients are too disturbed or too inward-looking to be able to do this for themselves.

Nurses need to be open enough to share their doubts, worries, and sometimes very strong negative countertransference feelings with their colleagues, to allow for the possibility of support for themselves and for an understanding of their patients to develop. Nurses need to develop the capacity to review their own behaviour, feelings, and needs and view them as important, both to themselves and to their patients. They need to take themselves seriously, as people and as professionals, and see psychosocial nursing as separate from, yet complementary to, the work of other therapists in the therapeutic process.

DeLambert (1982) noted that one of the most important aspects of the therapeutic community approach at the Cassel is an attempt to offer real, rather than contrived, responsibilities for patients and staff. For example, if one of the patients who is due to prepare breakfast for the whole of the community fails to get up in the morning to undertake this task, his or her absence has an immediate effect on other people, and this means that the missing patient is looked for. Other patients and nurses want to understand what the problem is, why the patient has not got up. The patient's absence is important, and this fact is fed back directly to the individual concerned.

Taking on real responsibility offers the chance of real success and or failure. Patients often fear failure to such an extent that it inhibits their ability to set even potentially achievable goals. Thus, one role of the nurse is to provide a space in which people can take risks, try things out, perhaps learn how to play in a supportive environment. Even if patients feel that they have let other people down, or have hurt and upset other patients or members of staff, they are helped to see that there is always the opportunity to try again and that it is possible to make reparations. One of the main tasks of psychosocial nursing is to design, maintain, facilitate, and monitor such opportunities.

Nurses' interact with the patients in an "everyday" way, developing relationships that enable the nurses and patients to share in activities and also allow for exchanges in ideas and thoughts. The hospital attempts to nurture a culture of openness and questioning, to allow for the often powerful feelings between people to be expressed, and to give space for these feelings to be thought about and understood. It is usual, therefore, that the nurse spends much more time with the patients than do most other professionals. Nurses are required to exercise great sensitivity and skill in their work with patients; they need to develop the capacity, as appropriate, to stand back and let things happen and to resist the urge to take over.

Being involved in these ways leads the nurses into particularly close relationships with the patients, which for the latter are often reminiscent of early childhood experiences within their families. This can put a nurse in a significant and sometimes difficult position of being experienced by the patient in ways related to early infantile patterns of experience, with important figures in the family. However, there needs to be the freedom for a patient's neurotic illness to be expressed and explored, for destructive and reparative behaviour, and for the chaos and disturbance that the patient is prone to re-enact and re-create to be repeated with the staff and patients around them. The feeling that headway is being made in an area of work—beginning to see the light—may abruptly change to an experience that someone has turned the light out. When to intervene is often in the minds of nurses: When will I understand? How can I tolerate this relationship? When will things change? At times, when engaged in a particularly difficult piece of work with a patient who seems to be making it clear that he or she regards working with the nurse as a waste of time and effort, a question in the nurse's mind may be, "When can I find another job?"!

In order for such disturbance both to emerge and to be contained, it is important that the patients are able to experience the hospital as an institution that has a degree of safety, continuity, and coherence in its direction, its practices, and its organization. Patients are extremely sensitive to the hospital staff's problems in working together, and success in treatment may depend to some extent on how hospital staff are able to achieve an integrated approach to the work—how well they are able to integrate their own working difficulties, as well as those generated through their dynamic interactions with patients.

Patients are admitted on to one of three individual units in the hospital. To an extent, these individual units have their own identities, their own staff teams, and differing ways of carrying out their work. The Patients' Pantry, which is the setting for the work described below, is directly managed by the two community nurses.

The Patients' Pantry

When the Cassel Hospital first moved to its current location, patients' meals were cooked by professional staff. At a later stage when the numbers of catering staff were reduced, patients' suppers were cooked during the day and then sent upstairs to be reheated in the evening by patients and nurses. About eighteen years ago, patients became involved in cooking suppers and devising menus, but they had no responsibility for the budget. All the food was stored in the professional staff's storage areas, and patients and nurses ordered ingredients for meals, with the ingredients being measured out and sent up by the catering staff. Any leftovers would be sent downstairs to be dealt with by the professional staff, who would transform these into tasty dishes to be served up the next day at lunch-time. On account of this, patients had very little responsibility for the consequences of wastage, which might occur for a number of reasons—for example, a dull meal or people not turning up for supper.

The original aims for the Patients' Pantry were:

1.   To allow nurses and patients to take increased responsibility for the feeding of the community apart from lunch, which would continue to be provided by professional cooks.

2. To allow more flexibility and creativity within the catering arrangements in the hospital.

3. To increase the therapeutic potential of all activities relating to the feeding of the community and to allow access and control over the community using the opportunities presented to nurses and patients by working together in these activities.

4. To exploit the regularity, frequency, and urgency of the need for food and to create a structure that as well as enhancing therapeutic activity in the hospital would, in itself, have a binding influence within the hospital.

Clinical examples

The author left the Cassel Hospital and the Pantry for nine months to take maternity leave, and the patient personnel in the Pantry had changed completely on her return. The three patients in the Pantry workgroup now included Amanda, a 36-year-old woman, eight months into her stay at the Cassel. She had presented to her GP complaining of distressing physical symptoms and feeling anxious. This was precipitated by a series of losses and bereavements in her close relationships. Her physical symptoms were thoroughly investigated, and Amanda had accepted that these might have been psychological in origin. What emerged in her therapy was a deep feeling of anger with her mother, who had left the family when Amanda was 14; subsequently Amanda had been divided in her loyalties between father and mother.

Another patient in the Pantry work group was a 26-year-old called Barbara, who had been admitted relatively recently. She had sought help in order to change her life, having been living with her parents and unable to work because of long-standing phobic and interpersonal anxieties.

The third member of the workgroup was a 24-year-old mother from the Families Unit called Teresa. Teresa had a 2½-year-old son called John. Teresa and John had been admitted to the Cassel Hospital five months previously. Prior to admission at the hospital, John had been placed with foster carers and his mother had served a short prison term in connection with the death of her younger daughter. They had been admitted to hospital in order to be assessed, with a view to Teresa regaining care and control of her child. In this family it was of key importance that staff at the hospital be able to make a clear and accurate assessment of the relationship between the mother and child, and to assess clearly the mother's ability to care for the child physically and emotionally whilst also making her own personal life and relationships.

AMANDA

In discussion with Amanda on my return to the workgroup, she told me that she thought little of her role in the Pantry, feeling that it was a meaningless job, which required little from her in terms of intellectual or emotional input. On exploration, it became apparent that it was not simply the job she had in the Pantry that she felt like this about. This had also happened in every job she had held prior to admission—very quickly she became disillusioned and did not feel that the job was of any value. The underlying sense was that she was too good for the positions she had taken on.

I took Amanda's criticisms and concerns about her role in the Pantry seriously. I engaged in discussion with her and other members of the Pantry Workgroup to try to think how her job could be made to feel more creative or worthwhile for her. However, it became apparent that every suggestion that was made, either by myself or anyone else, was quickly rebuffed. Her primary nurse told me that the main reason she wanted Amanda to work in the Pantry was because in her previous workgroup she had shown a marked inability to work co-operatively with other people. The nurse had thought that working in the Pantry (a small, interdependent workgroup) might put her in a position where she might have to own some of these feelings as having something to do with herself and to explore them, rather than just project all the negative, useless, hopeless feelings onto others or onto the institution of the hospital.

Amanda began to "act out" (Chiesa, 1989) in a major way around the Pantry, and it was noticeable that this acting out was related to my presence. For example, on a number of occasions she did not attend workgroup in the morning when we had made an agreement to undertake a particular piece of work. At first, when I raised this with her, she denied that her inability to get on with the job had anything to do with her relationship with me, but after perseverance on my part she eventually told me she thought I was bossy, domineering, did not really listen to her anyway, and also had my own opinion and ideas about things, so there was not much point in her trying to work with me. She softened this statement somewhat by saying that it was not just me, that she always found working with women difficult.

The issue of Amanda not getting up or not being available to participate in her workgroup on a regular basis came to a head one morning when she was due to issue an order for the children's teas to the nurse-manager and patient-manager of Children's Teas. When one of the mothers realized that her order had not been completed and Amanda had arrived late, in a slightly dishevelled state, the mother expressed her fury in no uncertain terms. Amanda's initial reaction was to blame me. She said that I should have got on with the order in her absence. The mother did not accept this at all, saying that the whole point of Amanda working in the Pantry was that she would take on some responsibility for herself and be aware of how her actions affected other people. She pointed out very forcibly that the people who were going to suffer, as a result of Amanda's not attending workgroup on time, were the children. The mention of children clearly upset Amanda, and I intervened at this point, saying that perhaps she and I could negotiate and get the order completed and deliver it.

I used this opportunity to talk to Amanda about the obvious difficulties that she was having working in the Pantry, and in particular the difficulty she seemed to be having in her relationship with me. She told me that she was having difficulties in working in the Pantry with me since she saw me as a bad mother, having left my baby to come back to work. This hurt! My instant impulse was to explain to her my intricate childcare arrangements. However, I managed to avoid doing this and instead acknowledged that it was useful that she had told me how she felt. We carried on with the task and got the order completed.

No revolutionary change happened in Amanda's working relationship in the Pantry following this, but it did feel that she began to settle into the job, tolerating more the inevitable routines and even being able to use some of the opportunities to show her own creativity, such as reorganizing the storage space for the dry goods and drawing up a list of new hardware that it would be useful for the Pantry to have.

Amanda had begun to learn to tolerate anxiety about possible faults both in herself and in the situation at hand. In this, as described by Erikson (1950), she was increasingly able to experience satisfaction from her exercising of responsibility. Amanda experienced a sense that what she did in relation to her work in the Pantry actually mattered to other people. She also discovered that she could have very negative critical feelings about me as a person and yet still work cooperatively with me as a colleague. She also began to work more cooperatively with the other members of the workgroup, even making us all a cup of tea on occasion, although for her this meant the end of work—because she was adamant that she could not drink tea and work at the same time.

BARBARA

Two weeks after my return to the hospital and the Pantry Workgroup, the other community nurse with whom I worked went away on leave. Amanda's attendance and ability to get on with the job in the Pantry at this time was very inconsistent. Barbara and I became the only consistent members of the Pantry Workgroup for at least a couple of weeks, and Barbara proved herself to be conscientious, creative, reliable, and an all-round "good egg".

I found myself feeling very grateful that she was working with me in the Pantry. She could use her own initiative, and I experienced her as an emotionally generous and quietly humorous individual. However, her behaviour changed markedly once the workgroup became more settled and stable, as other people joined us and were reliable there. She became ungiving, grudging, often uncommunicative, resentful of assistance yet angry if she did not receive it. She felt like a different person. It was clear that in a one-to-one relationship with me, Barbara was able to show more of her true potential, creativity, and humour, but she found it very difficult to share these attributes with more than one person at a time. This rigid way of functioning was also reflected in the way she did her job. She looked after the milk, bread, and dairy order in the Pantry. It became apparent that Barbara found all this very difficult to do. She made others feel that they were imposing on her or expecting too much from her, even when they made no requests that deviated from the usual, in terms of ordering. It was as if Barbara's creativity and ability to play was split off from her habitual way of relating to other people.

I talked to the rest of the workgroup about my experience of working with Barbara when we were on our own together, but I wondered whether people believed me because it seemed so alien to the Barbara who was part of the group. She herself would never confirm or deny anything I said, which seemed to relate to the more creative side of herself. Sadly, in my remaining time in the Pantry, I never really gained any real sense of working in a creative or cooperative way with Barbara. Barbara also found it sad, irritating, and frustrating that she could not share more of herself with other people.

Barbara continued to work in the Pantry for a few months. The nurses and patients who worked closely with her continued to feel angry and frustrated at times with her inability to share positive aspects of herself with them. Her creativity did begin to show itself again, but in ways that were generally perceived as negative. She went through periods of under-ordering the required commodities, and, after she was tackled about this by the nurses, she reversed the situation and began to over-order. This I felt was a positive step for Barbara in as much as it brought her relationships with work, her workgroup colleagues, and the remainder of the community very much more to life.

Winnicott said: "To control what is outside one, one has to do things, not simply to think or to wish, and doing things takes time. Playing is doing." It seems to me that, with her acting out, Barbara was at least being able to play. I quote again, "Play is universal, and belongs to health. Playing facilitates growth and therefore health, play leads into group relationships. Playing is a form of communication with others" (Winnicott, 1970).

TERESA

Teresa's job in the Pantry was to manage the vegetables. This involved having access to vegetable price lists (which were supplied to us on a weekly basis by the greengrocer) and choosing appropriate quantities of vegetables at an appropriate price. It was notable, when she began work in the pantry, that Teresa always made sure that her son John was supplied with plenty of things to do. At first John would always arrive at the workgroup with crayons and colouring books, or cars, Lego, etc. As with any child of his age, John quickly became interested in what his mother was doing, rather than what he was supposed to be doing himself. Teresa found this very difficult to deal with, feeling that she could not manage to entertain her son at the same time as getting on with doing her work. Very quickly we found that John stopped coming with his mother to the workgroup, and that other patients who were working elsewhere would take responsibility for John and actually involve him in their work—for example, letting him sweep the floors and polish tables. This clearly defeated the object of our trying to help Teresa manage to look after her child and to play with her child at the same time as getting on with doing constructive work herself.

Once the issue was raised with her, however, Teresa sullenly and resentfully made sure that John was in her care during workgroup time. John, who was a gregarious, precocious little boy, quickly developed a habit of helping me to take out the rubbish and put it in the bins. (He also helped Barbara to pack away the dry goods, sorting the cupboard out neatly and counting the number of cereal packets.) However, he still did not spend much time actually working or playing with his mother. Teresa herself undertook her job very conscientiously. She got over her initial feeling of being on trial and began actually to enjoy the work. She admitted that she preferred John to be looked after by other people, as this allowed her the freedom to get on with her work. Her biggest fear, however, was that John would have a tantrum and would somehow show her up to be a not–good-enough mother.

Teresa had no difficulty with the work that she had to do with the workgroup. She had no difficulty in relating to other members of the workgroup. She did, however, have major difficulties in relating to her child and including her child in the work. We tackled this issue by working with Teresa and helping her to include John. John started by helping his mother weigh the vegetables. From being very tentative and scared of involving her son in the work, Teresa began to take more and more pride in her son's achievements. John quickly learnt the names of all the vegetables, the colour of all the fruit, where everything went, and took great delight in ordering other people around and making sure they did things properly as well.

The process of change was not totally smooth, and there were times when the nurses in the workgroup particularly were concerned about Teresa's ability to relate to her son and about John's pseudo-adult presentation. Generally, however, the process of working in the Pantry, and having a space and a prescribed task that they could achieve together, proved to be a very helpful and creative experience for mother and son.

Conclusion

The Patients' Pantry is a structure that has a time, a place, and a purpose. Inherent in this structure is an opportunity for play. Inherent in play is the opportunity for people to be creative. Winnicott (1970) says: "It is creative apperception more than anything else that makes the individual feel that life is worth living.

Contrasted with this is a relationship to external reality which is one of compliance, the world and its details being recognized, but only as something to be fitted in with or demanding adaptation."

Compliance carries with it a sense of futility for the individual, and it is associated with the idea that nothing matters and that life is not worth living. Tantalizingly, many patients have experienced just enough creative living to recognize that for most of the time they are living uncreatively, as if caught up in the creativity of someone else. Assuming that the patient is able to understand and carry out the tasks inherent in the life of the community, everything that happens is potentially creative. Environmental factors, however, reinforce personal aspects that stifle or constrain the latent creative processes.

Individuals either live creatively and find that life is worth living, or else they cannot live creatively and are doubtful about the value of living. The clinical examples presented in this chapter show how a structure like the Patients' Pantry can provide a "potential space" in which individuals' difficulties in playing and being creative can be registered—at times, repeatedly registered. Nurses, using the whole gamut of professional skills, can get alongside patients, helping them to take risks and assisting them to be able to play, sometimes it seems for the first time.

CHAPTER FOUR

The use of leisure activities in psychosocial practice

Graham McCaffrey

In this chapter I explore the use of social and leisure activities as part of psychosocial practice within the therapeutic programme of the Cassel Hospital.

The hospital uses a treatment model somewhat different from that of most other therapeutic communities, but it shares with them some essential attributes, as described by Kennard (1983, pp. 7–8):

1. an informal, communal atmosphere;
2. the central place of group meetings in the therapeutic programme;
3. sharing the work of maintaining and running the community;
4. the recognition of patients or residents as auxiliary therapists, commenting on and influencing each other's behaviour and attitudes;
5. a motivating belief in the value of psychodynamic processes as agents for enquiry and personal change.

Nurses have a central role: working with patients in facilitating groups, doing practical tasks, and running many community functions alongside them. Patients are involved by co-managing with nurses aspects of community life. These include (as Flynn suggested in Chapter 3) ordering food, arranging rotas for cooking and cleaning, and responding to patients who appear very distressed or at risk of harming themselves or others. In the course of this close work with patients, nurses develop an awareness of patients' difficulties as they emerge.

A patient in a daily cleaning group, for example, took on more and more of the work, cleaning the kitchen excessively but not allowing others to share responsibility. This was questioned and discussed by nurses both while it was happening and in subsequent community meetings. The patient was thus enabled to re-examine her behaviour and talk about her fear of losing control over feelings of anger and despair, which she was driving away through frantic activity. Through this process she was helped to come to a more mutual, shared approach towards working with others.

Nursing interventions and outcomes are assessed by peer-group discussion and coordinated with the patient's psycho-therapist in the multidisciplinary team. By using the knowledge and understanding gained through such interactions, nurses attempt to formulate collaborative individual treatment plans with patients. One dimension of the nursing approach is to express spontaneous and honest emotional responses to patients. This has always to be tempered by judgements about what is professionally appropriate and by the therapeutic need, at all times leaving open a space for further dialogue with patients. Such an approach incorporates a notion of normative social and emotional expectations—for example, expectations that people turn up to do a job they have agreed to do unless they have given a good reason not to, or that shock, upset, and anger are realistic responses to the sight of self-inflicted wounds. The idea of the normative in the community also incorporates some individual variation so that, although nurses share a common core approach, they do not adhere to a uniform set of ideas and responses. The emphasis on socially normative routines, activities, and behaviours supports a manifest conceptualization of the therapeutic community as a microcosm of its surrounding society. But it is an environment that is contained and, to a degree, protected in order to allow patients, many with severe difficulties, to cope with an emotionally testing and anxiety-provoking treatment.

Activities

The use of activities is one part of our nurses' work. The term "activities" denotes a particular segment of the social microcosm: namely, voluntary, social, and leisure activities. There are a number of reasons why activities are accorded a high value and importance within the therapeutic programme. In the social-microcosm aspect of a therapeutic community, they simply form part of a normative idea that a balanced and satisfactory life involves both work and leisure. Patients invariably have difficulties in both of these aspects of social life. Beyond this, because the community also requires inquiry and self-reflection about feelings and behaviour, it is also important to work out a thoroughgoing rationale for activities so that patients and staff can see how they can become an active element in therapeutic work.

The word "activities" describes things that people might ordinarily do in the space of leisure time outside their working hours. These include cultural activities such as painting, going to the theatre, or reading poetry; sport and exercise such as badminton, aerobics, swimming; indoor games such as chess, pool, table tennis. My own clinical experience was of running, with a patient, a poetry-reading group.

Activities in the hospital are not exactly the same as those that people do in leisure time at home. In the hospital, social and leisure activities must have active, social, and managed elements. Watching television, for example, takes up a large part of many people's free time, but it is not an activity within the therapeutic programme. By a fine distinction, however, there is a video activity. The difference is that the selection and showing of a video film requires an individual to take some responsibility—to make a choice of film, to negotiate and maintain boundaries of time and venue, and to try to drum up some interest in a shared experience.

> The element of choice within this activity of managing the video activity became a focus for clinical work with an adolescent patient who took on the job. He was very socially withdrawn and inexpressive, yet harboured violent fantasies by which he sometimes felt troubled. He undermined the principle of working with a nurse by arranging video viewing nights at times other than those agreed. In addition, without consulting anyone else, he rented films with violent content that were disturbing to some other patients. Thus, his involvement with the activity had distinct social implications that provided a source of therapeutic work. His behaviour was questioned by nurses and by other patients, encouraging him to think about possible connections between his private fantasies and his actions in the social world of the hospital.

The social dimension of activities is, therefore, one of the keys to their therapeutic usefulness in meeting the needs of individual patients and in providing points of therapeutic intervention.

Organizational context

The distinction between what is and is not an activity becomes clearer when it is placed in the context of the therapeutic community's structures. The hospital (unlike many other therapeutic communities) has all sorts of subdivisions within it. It is divided into three units—for single adults, for families, and for adolescents. There is also a division of labour between psychotherapists, who see patients for individual and group psychotherapy, and nurses, whose psychosocial practice centres on facilitating and participating in everyday work such as cooking, cleaning, and leisure activities. Patients might choose to talk about activities in a therapy session, but these discussions come primarily within the sphere of the nursing work.

Leisure activities are part of the remit of the community team, which administers the supra-unit aspects of the therapeutic community. In other words, activities are open to patients from all the units and can provide opportunities for working with a wider range of people. The activities are overseen by a committee of patients, elected by the patients. The committee consists of a chairperson, treasurer, and secretary, and they work with one of the two nurses from the community team. There is no fixed term for committee members to serve, although they usually continue in one of the jobs for about three months. It is important to try to keep in mind the relevance and usefulness of the job in pursuing their individual treatment aims; for example, an aim might be to look at a patient's pattern of avoidance of regular responsibility, or to encourage him or her to explore the value of social activities if he or she has been very isolated.

In addition to chairing the weekly activities meeting, the activities chairperson also attends a weekly meeting in which other senior staff and patient representatives discuss issues affecting the community. This latter function reflects the importance attached to the state of activities within the hospital. The wish and capacity of patients to be together and to do things voluntarily together, or its opposite extreme, social isolationism, can be used as a measure of the social cohesion—or the level of disturbance—within the patients' group.

The treasurer keeps track of the annual budget for activities and of a weekly fund for sundries such as newspapers. Decisions about funding requests are made by the whole committee and by the nurse working with them.

The secretary takes minutes of the weekly meeting, types them, and presents copies at the next meeting.

Therapeutic possibilities arise from a patient undertaking the secretary's or the treasurers role, mundane though such tasks may at first appear. For example, issues of budgeting, trust, and giving to others may take on a specific meaning and usage to the individual patient who takes it on. At a level of basic skills, patients with poor literacy have used the job of secretary to practise listening and writing skills; with careful attention from a nurse, the job offers a venue where anxiety and feelings of shame about poor literacy skills can be shared and worked upon and thereby reduced.

At a more complex emotional level, one young woman doing the secretary's job regularly failed to present the minutes. She either did not write them at all, or she destroyed the finished copy before the weekly meeting. Observation of this pattern by the activities nurse led to it being discussed among the committee. It emerged that the patient had such a fear of any error being seen by others that she would avoid presenting her minutes to the meeting. It was then arranged that one other patient, with whom she felt safe, would look at the minutes with her and reassure her about her work, which, in reality, was of a high standard. Once this plan was implemented, the patient was able, with increasing confidence, to present the minutes and test out her anxiety against the reality that other people were more interested in using the minutes in the meeting than in scouring them for minor mistakes.

The weekly activities meeting, convened by the committee, nurse, and community doctor, is open to all patients and nurses. People usually attend because they manage an activity. Each separate activity is run by a nurse and a patient-manager. It is up to them to initiate the activity, to establish a time and a venue for it, and to make requests for any funding that they think they may need. Money can be used for anything from a new table-tennis ball to theatre tickets, or from pottery clay to purchasing CDs.

Social and therapeutic purpose

Different categories of activity can present scope for work with problems that patients may have in particular areas of functioning. Activities can have both positive attributes and countervailing psychological obstacles. I offer three examples.

Physical activities

Swimming and exercise improve fitness and provide a sense of physical well-being. They can enhance confidence through learning and demonstrating a skill, which gives a sense of physical freedom and coordination.

However, there is also an emotional domain that can be acknowledged by the nurse in talking with patients about their (the patients') experience of such activities and sharing their own feelings and attitudes towards their own bodies and/or their feelings about other people's bodies. For example, if a female patient bears scars from self-mutilation, undressing to go swimming might help her to face up to other people's reaction to her behaviour.

A patient, with a long history of anorexia and who exercised excessively to burn off calories, wished to manage an aerobics activity. There was open discussion as to the advisability of this for her, with conflicting opinions expressed among the staff team. In the end, the activity went ahead with the aim of performing relatively gentle exercises. The patient's primary nurse monitored her weight with her to ensure that it did not fall below a medically determined minimum level. The possibility of a harmful effect of the activity was thus balanced against the social and fitness benefits that it provided at the same time, for the patient and others.

Poetry reading

Poetry reading allows one, literally, to speak out. It calls into play an appreciation of language, rhythm, critical intelligence, and personal taste. It is a venue for an imaginative freedom in response to emotionally charged language that can at times feel exposing. Difficulties in undertaking social activity that may become available for treatment include anxiety about revealing something of one's inner emotional world and anxiety about performing in front of others.

The first patient-manager of the poetry reading group used the emotional force present in poetry to memorable effect. He kicked off the opening meeting of the group by reading Larkin's poem, "This Be The Verse", which begins "They fuck you up, your mum and dad" (1974). He took the opportunity, appropriately, to use something which gave vent to a feeling of his own.

A later patient-manager of the group was preoccupied with Byronic fantasies about her nurse co-manager; as a result, she tried to exclude other patients from the group. Her wish to let fantasy push out the reality of her role, as a group leader, had to be tactfully pointed out. This example raises again the crucial inter-personal and social aspect of activities. For the patient, this episode brought up questions about her previous social isolation and why she feared and resented social contact outside the comfortable illusion of an imagined intimacy.

Bicycle maintenance

Bicycle maintenance requires dexterity and technical skill, which includes a conscientiousness about finishing a job properly. This tests the intrapsychic reparative capacity of an individual, by means of actual repair to a machine. Jaques (1960, p. 360) describes this as an element in all work.

Emergence of self in relation to others through activities

A useful dimension in all kinds of activities is taking pride in one's talents and the capacity to allow others to see them. For people with low self-esteem, this can be a difficult but valuable thing to achieve; it entails distinguishing oneself within, or from, the group of patients and thereby risking losing a place within it. This means potentially having to overcome the safe but often stifling inertia of the pseudo-mutual group (Gustafson, 1976, p. 992), which pre-tends that there are no differences within it in order to maintain a false stability. I observed this happening in the poetry group with a patient-manager who struggled against making any decisions (e.g. about which new books to buy) when working with me. She continually tried to involve the rest of the group in order to avoid distinguishing herself as the designated patient-manager.

Another component of activities is the ability to play. Play is an important part of childhood development; when such development has been impaired, an adult can find it painfully difficult to relax, have fun, and be playful. The community's activities offer a series of spaces in which to play in a safe environment. The idea of play can be extended to include an element in creative tasks such as painting or sculpting. These have a laborious and serious side to them, but they also require a playfulness in the sense of being able to imagine disparate elements transformed into a new whole. This is equivalent to the component of work which Jaques calls "lysis and scanning". There must be a plasticity in mental process to synthesize the available conscious and unconscious elements pertaining to a task. If, however, "the mental process is concrete and inflexible, the bits and particles are not available for synthesis" (Jaques, 1960. p. 360), and no new integration of elements can emerge.

Activities enable people to encounter each other in ways different from those determined by their usual work roles. This happens in patient–patient interactions but even more so in patient–nurse interactions. An extreme example is the hospital's annual Christmas revue, written and performed by nurses and patients together. This invariably includes some satirical digs at the institution and permits patients and nurses to dress up and act in outrageous characterizations together. There is often a literal role reversal, with patients taking the part of nurses and vice-versa. Participants on either side are able to express some of the things that they envy, are jealous of, dislike, or are amused by in the other. These, of course, are secrets to no one, but are usually only tacitly understood. Nurses can act out their jealousy of what they sometimes experience, such as the patient's freedom to refuse to join in community life; conversely, patients can adopt the persona of the nurse, who, as they sometimes experience, is always in the right.

To a lesser degree, this experience of seeing oneself and others differently is present in all activities. For example, a nurse might be battling with a patient in a morning meeting to try to gethim to talk about why he had not helped cook supper the night before; in the afternoon the same nurse and patient could be battling it out in a game of table tennis. These are quite different moments for each participant in the same relationship. The nurturing of such experiences enables patients (and nurses) to be aware of the possibility of seeing different parts of others and of themselves, and leads to the toleration and appreciation of diversity in relationships. The development of opportunities for such experiences is at the core of psychosocial nursing.

Voluntary space

A crucial point about activities, which underpins all the other considerations, is that they make use of voluntary space. In the social analogy, this is free time, as opposed to work time, or, as Mark Twain puts it in Tom Sawyer, "Work consists of whatever a body is obliged to do, and play consists of whatever a body is not obliged to do" (1976). The voluntary nature of activities lends them an important dimension as part of treatment. Jaques (1960) discusses the ego strength that is required to perform a task, in order to bear the uncertainty of its outcome and to contain the intrapsychic and real separating out and reintegration of parts of a task.

In most parts of the therapeutic programme, there is an institutional obligation to perform a task. The rota to cook supper for the community, for example, carries considerable weight in the community, and peer pressure among patients is the main instrument of its enforcement. In this case, there is a powerful external containment (in the form of peer pressure) for processing the task. By contrast, in activities there is far less external containment and the consequences of failure to carry out a task are far less severe. The badminton activity not taking place will have far less impact on the community than the supper not being cooked. It may be argued, therefore, that activities can offer more of a testing ground of a patient's capacity to work in Jaques' sense. The performance of the task is less bounded and supported by external structures and, consequently, is more dependent on the patient's own internal ego-strength.

In practice, patient and nurse co-managers will encourage their peers to join in an activity, say a game of football. The co-managers invariably feel an emotional investment in the game being successful because they have provided an impetus and wish for it to happen. The significance of ego strength operating in voluntary space applies particularly to the individuals in this situation. In arranging the game, they have summoned up internal psychological resources, such as the capacity to hold to the idea of a successful realization of the wished-for game. In doing this they have been able to contain their fears that no one else will want to play and that they will feel rejected, or that people will play but not enjoy themselves and that they will feel resented. If an unconscious destructive urge on the managers' part has not got in the way, they will also have assembled the physical resources of ball, field, and goalposts. When such efforts are undertaken out of one's own wishes and imagination, and not because one has been told to undertake them, there is a self-affirming quality (even if the activity was only partially successful). Patients' involvement in voluntary activities can stimulate the inherent potential for feelings of self-worth and pleasure that can be difficult to reach in more formalized areas of clinical work.

In the hospital, there is a discernible cycle in activities: a period of enthusiasm followed by one of disillusionment and apathy. The task falls to the managers of the activity, both nurse and patient, either to look for ways of sustaining it and trying to re-awaken interest or to let it slide into disuse and end it. Many objective factors influence the outcome: whether the patient is soon to leave the hospital, other commitments on the part of the patient-manager or the nurse-manager—even the time of year can be important if it is a seasonal sport. But it is also a question at such times of the degree of value and commitment that they continue to attach to the activity when they know that they do not have to do it.

However, the notion of voluntary space in a therapeutic community is problematic, and the analogy of leisure time can, at a certain point, no longer apply. For patients, the inclusiveness of a therapeutic community blurs the line between work and leisure. Leisure activities undoubtedly feel different from other parts of treatment, but they are still done with the same people in the same building and are still subject to the therapeutic eye. This is different from the work/leisure dichotomy in everyday life, where there are generally much clearer distinctions of time, place, and participants between the two.

The complexity is even more marked for nurses. They are encouraged to take on managing and participating in activities for which they feel some personal enthusiasm, and yet they also have to do them because it is part of their job. There is a paradox that activities must be voluntary—otherwise an essential point about them is lost—and yet they must be done because they represent an essential part of life, and an obligatory part of the nurse's role.

In practice, this is worked out uneasily. Nurse-managers become frustrated with junior nurses if they are not undertaking an activity, and nurses struggle perennially to find time to do so. The institution compounds the difficulty by fixing the times and venues of a plethora of meetings. It is difficult to find free spaces in the timetabled day in which to hold activities, since in this respect they maintain their voluntary identity. Sometimes they are pushed into "free" time after the end of the nurse's working day. I used to do this with the poetry reading group, because it was the only way I felt able to concentrate on it and to leave my other duties. This indicates the lower priority that nurses end up giving to activities as opposed to other parts of their role and also, I suggest, some ambivalence or confusion about mixing "work" and "leisure".

Conclusion

I have discussed some of the therapeutic possibilities of leisure activities in nursing disturbed patients. One recurring theme is the social dimension of activities: they offer a milieu of relating with other people in a freer way than is possible in more task-oriented or role-defined settings. The anxiety engendered by less-defined space is offset by the stakes of success and failure being lowered. The possibilities of patients developing a sense of social being within activities counters the social isolation that has often been a long-established feature of their lives. A second fundamental theme is the possibility of creative self-expression and self-affirmation in all kinds of leisure activity, and not only those, such as art and writing, that we first think of as creative. This runs counter to the self-destructive forms of expression that, again, have often long been a pattern of patients' lives.

This chapter has looked at activities, in a specialized sense, as part of the psychosocial practice of nurses at the Cassel Hospital. This is a specific area, but I believe that wider points for nurses and others can be drawn from it. When rehabilitation is the purpose of care, different tasks may have different social meanings that can influence the carer–patient relationship and the carer's own attitude to work. Goals in treatment can be related to particular activities—both the social equivalents of activities within the treatment setting and with regard to the tasks involved and their specific therapeutic potential.

CHAPTER FIVE

The therapeutic ingredients of baking a cake

Fritha Irwin

I would like to describe the therapeutic opportunities that presented themselves to one particular patient, Elizabeth, whilst she was in treatment at the Cassel Hospital, through her involvement with me in the everyday task of baking cakes.

As part of the therapeutic programme, various social and leisure activities are on offer to the patients, mostly during unstructured time in the afternoon and evening. They are optional, but patients are encouraged to join activities or to take on responsibility for a specific activity and manage it. Each activity is managed jointly by a nurse and a patient. Activities are overseen by an activities committee. There are a variety of activities on offer; in the recent past these have included pottery, art, drama, a band, singing, swimming, badminton, table tennis, and a cake-baking activity.

An important part of the philosophy of our work at the Cassel Hospital is to maintain the expectation that patients can function as responsible adults despite their often evident disturbance. By encouraging them to take on a responsibility within the community, such as managing an activity, staff demonstrate this expectation and a belief that, whatever their state, patients also have functioning capacities. If the activity is successful, patients gain enjoyment and self-confidence. When it is unsuccessful, the reasons for this will be enquired into by the nurse and the patient-manager, along with the activities committee. It may be that other patients have little interest in this particular activity or that it clashes in time with other commitments. Often, the failure is connected with how the patient-manager relates to others—by being aggressive, intimidating, or controlling, for example. Once these difficulties are identified, the patient has the opportunity to change, thus gaining therapeutically.

The activity managers are expected to be reliable and responsible about organizing their activity. They may at times feel distressed and want to "collapse"; our culture in the hospital would encourage them not to regress and give up but to obtain support from others in order to continue with everyday life. Patients who have been looking forward to joining the activity may apply peer pressure, which will also encourage the manager to continue to function.

By being involved in an activity, the patients have the opportunity to form and experience new relationships in a relaxed way.

Activities can be fun! Much of our treatment programme is intense and serious, so a space for lighter moments and relaxation is an important balance to the everyday work. Patients can also learn to socialize and develop social skills. They have the chance to demonstrate and develop their creativity, as well as being given the opportunity to play.

Skills gained from involvement in activities can be internalized and used in the outside world: the skill to work and negotiate with others, the skill to manage a realistic budget, the skill of developing interests and hobbies, for example.

As most activities occur during time outside the formal treatment structure, the groups are also of value in helping the community, as a whole, to contain anxiety and disturbance when there are fewer staff members around. Patients are encouraged to share their distress with others and to receive support. Through this mutual process, feelings that initially seemed overwhelming become contained and manageable.

ELIZABETH

I would now like to consider the therapeutic gains made by Elizabeth, with whom I managed the cake-making activity for approximately seven months.

Elizabeth was a 39-year-old divorced woman on the adult unit. She had three children but had had little contact with them for several years. On admission, Elizabeth was living in a Mind group home; she received state benefits and was doing a word-processing course but had not worked in paid employment for some years.

She came from a very deprived background, with a history of physical, verbal, and sexual abuse. At the age of 9 years she was taken into care, and for the next six years she was moved constantly from one children's home to another. During one of these placements, she was sexually abused by a member of staff. At age 15, she returned to live with her parents and was subjected to further sexual abuse by her father. This was never openly discussed in the family. To escape this situation, Elizabeth left home at 18 and shortly afterwards married an abusive, violent man, who fathered her three children. Marriage to this aggressive partner repeated her experience of being abused, and she again solved the situation by leaving, rather than confronting it. Her children stayed with their father.

Elizabeth entered treatment at the Cassel Hospital in 1994 with a long history of depression and self-destructive behaviour. She was known to be physically violent; she cut herself and had taken serious overdoses. However, one of her main strengths was her wish to change, her motivation in wanting to face up to difficult issues in order to move on in her life. She did, indeed, work hard in her treatment and used many therapeutic opportunities in order to facilitate change for herself. One of these opportunities was the way that she was willing to face issues that were raised for her during her turn as the cake-making activity manager.

After being in treatment for about two months, Elizabeth was being encouraged to become more involved in the community and to take on some responsibilities. She expressed an interest in the management of the cake-making activity, working with myself as the nurse-manager. Cake making was something that Elizabeth had previously enjoyed, but she had lost confidence in any of her abilities in the last few years. We discussed the timing of the activity and decided that it would take place on a Wednesday evening from 8 p.m. to 9 p.m., with the end result being served to the patient community during a community coffee get-together on Thursday evening. Elizabeth and I met regularly on a Monday to order the ingredients, discuss what would be cooked, and think together about how the activity was progressing and about Elizabeth's role as the activity manager. Although there were times during her treatment when Elizabeth was unable to fulfil her responsibilities in other areas, she never once failed to organize the cake-making activity, despite the difficulties she experienced with it.

I would now like to turn to the issues that emerged as the activity progressed.

As a result of the abuse she had received over many years, Elizabeth had little self-esteem and therefore little sense of having something good within her that she could offer to others. The cakes that she produced were a concrete way of offering something to other patients, and these were gratefully received. She was able to internalize this interaction and begin to believe that she did have the capacity to give to other people on an emotional level. Once she realized this, her natural warmth became much more visible and open, and her genuine caring side was able to flourish.

Her husband had cruelly criticized her cooking during the time that they were together, resulting in a complete loss of confidence in her capacities to cook. When she began to receive well-deserved compliments on her cooking, her self-confidence increased. It was extremely hard for her to accept these comments at face value, but over a period of time she began to trust others and thus believe what they were saying.

Elizabeth's past had made her wary of being hurt in relationships again, so as a defence she related in an aggressive and, at times, intimidating way. This meant that it was difficult for her to work with other people and to gain support for herself by sharing her distress. At first, she found it almost impossible to encourage other patients to join the activity and wanted to do it alone. Much of my work at this time was to explore this problem with her and to support her in inviting other patients to join the activity. With help, she was able to say why she kept people at a distance. Once others understood, they were able to challenge her aggressiveness and support the distress underneath.

She was also very controlling within the activity, as a way of keeping people away. As her relationships and trust improved, she became able to discuss the content of the activity with others, thus allowing them to express their ideas and creativity.

A further aspect to Elizabeth's difficulty in allowing others to join the activity may have been her unspoken wish to have an exclusive relationship with me.

Elizabeth's psychotherapist felt that Elizabeth's only way of making contact with other people was by presenting herself as a victim and by relating the story of her abuse, thus damaging her relationships. An important change, then, for Elizabeth to make, was for her to find the means of relating to others in ordinary social ways. Her involvement in the cake-making activity gave her a venue in which she was able to explore new, more acceptable ways of relating.

Another theme that emerged from Elizabeth's therapy sessions was her omnipotent sense of damaging others. At times, this fear made it extremely hard for her to present her cakes to the community as she felt concerned that she might poison them. By reality-testing this feeling she was able to realize that her fear was not based in reality, and she gained insight, through her therapy, into the fact that this damage to others might occur through her ways of relating.

Although Elizabeth had three children, she rarely mentioned them within the community. She felt enormous guilt at having abandoned them, and I wondered with her whether, by taking on a nurturing, feeding role within the community, she was trying to make some reparation for this abandonment.

Another significant omission from Elizabeth's treatment was any discussion about her mother. As we worked together on the cake-making activity, Elizabeth developed a maternal transference to me which, when explored verbally, enabled her to focus during therapy on her relationship to her mother. This was one of the most important areas of work for her during her time at the Cassel.

> The concept of transference refers to those occasions when the patient may act towards a member of staff as if she was a parental figure. If, for example, a patient responds to a nurse as if she was a loved or hated mother it may be difficult for them to develop an adult/adult co-operative relationship without these transference feelings getting in the way of the work they need to do together. [Chapman, 1984, p. 3]

Many times Elizabeth felt that she was ignored by and unimportant to me. Although she found these feelings hard to express, she did manage to tell me. During discussion it became apparent that the feelings were linked to her mother and, in particular, to her inability to protect Elizabeth from the abuse. Elizabeth's fury towards her mother also came in my direction on occasion, particularly when I went on annual leave. She felt abandoned by me (as she had been by her mother) and experienced me as totally uncaring (as her mother had been). On one occasion I forgot to collect the piece of cake that she always gave to me on the Friday morning. Her reaction to this mistake was out of all proportion to my offence, but, again, it was linked to her feelings of not being important or valued.

At other times I had a sense of Elizabeth wanting to please or placate me. I feel that her wish to avoid any expression of conflict or anger was, again, a result of a mother who had been harsh and judgemental on many occasions when Elizabeth was young.

As a result of Elizabeth's willingness to respond to a therapeutic opportunity, she became in touch with feelings about her mother that had previously been suppressed. She utilized her therapy sessions to explore this very painful area and to achieve some resolution.

My experience of working with Elizabeth was, overall, a warm one, although we did have some difficult times. I was impressed by her ability to use her insight and to take risks in utilizing therapeutic opportunities. She gained much from treatment and made positive changes.

I would like to conclude with Elizabeth's short account of her experience of managing the cake-making activity.

ELIZABETH'S ACCOUNT

"The cake-baking activity is one of many activities here at the Cassel Hospital for anybody and everybody to join in if they want to. It is not a structure, so taking part is purely voluntary, although it is the patient-manager's role to try and encourage other patients to do so.

"I myself managed the cake-baking activity for eight months, although generally a patient would probably only do an activity for about three to four months. I was reluctant to give it up as I got a great deal out of doing the cake-baking activity, as patients and staff were never short on complimenting the cakes that were made. But one of the reasons I didn't want to give it up was because I felt that without presenting the community with something worthwhile then I wasn't a worthy person, which was an issue for me. And I did get a big buzz out of presenting the cake to the community at Community Coffee. I also found it very hard to ask and encourage others to join in the activity, which included choosing a cake to be baked, as I felt like I was asking for something for myself, which I hated doing instead of other people supporting me and vice versa and also them getting something out of doing cake baking too. It wasn't that I didn't want people to participate in the cake baking, it was me finding it hard to accept support from others for myself.

"The number of people who attended varied from week to week. Sometimes there were four or five people participating and sometimes I did it on my own.

"There were also issues around my mother which I managed to confront with the nurse-manager, Fritha Irwin, which were difficult and painful.

"I had difficulties in working with people with the slightest authority, which was my view of the nurses. I felt that they were there to criticize rather than to encourage and support me in doing the activity, and because of this on occasion I became very angry with them.

"It was fun doing the activity with other patients, and it helped me in forming relationships and sometimes really getting to know people and listening to some of their difficulties. I learnt from them and I hope they learnt a lot from me too. It's helped build up my confidence and self-esteem in many areas and I hope it does the same for others who take on the cake-baking activity in the future."

REFERENCES

Barton, R. (1959). *Institutional Neurosis*. Bristol: John Wright.

Chapman, G. E. (1984). A therapeutic community, psychosocial nursing and the nursing process. *International Journal of Therapeutic Communities, 5*: 68–76.

Chiesa, M. (1989). Different origins and meanings of acute acting out in an inpatient setting. *Psychoanalytic Psychotherapy, 4* (2): 155–168.

Conran, M. (1984). The patient in hospital. *Psychoanalytic Psychotherapy, 1*: 31–43.

Dartington, A. (1994). Where angels fear to tread. In: A. Obholzer & V. Roberts (Eds.), *The Unconscious at Work*. London: Routledge.

DeLambert, L. (1982). The role of a nurse in a psychotherapeutic institution. In: *Psychotherapie in der Klinik*. Berlin: Springer-Verlag.

Denford, J., & Griffiths, P. (1993). "Transferences to the institution" and their effect on inpatient treatment at the Cassel Hospital. *Therapeutic Communities, 14* (4): 237–248.

Erikson, E. H. (1950). *Childhood and Society*. New York: W. W. Norton.

Freud, S. (1900a). *The Interpretation of Dreams. S.E.,* 4–5. London: Hogarth Press.

Freud, S. (1901b). *The Psychopathology of Everyday Life. S.E.,* 6. London: Hogarth Press.

Freud, S. (1911b). Formulations on the two principles of mental functioning. *S.E.,* 12. London: Hogarth Press.

Freud, S. (1913a). An evidential dream. *S.E.,* 12. London: Hogarth Press.

Gabbard, G. O. (1992). The therapeutic relationship in psychiatric hospital treatment. *Bulletin of the Menninger Clinic, 56* (1): 4–19.

Goffman, E. (1961). *Asylums*. Harmondsworth: Penguin Books.

Griffiths, P., & Leach, G. (1997). Psychosocial nursing: a model learnt from experience. In: E. Barnes, P. Griffiths, J. Ord, & D. Wells (Eds.), *Face to Face with Distress: The Professional Use of Self in Psychosocial Care*. London: Butterworth Heinemann.

Grunberg, S. (1979). Thinking and the development of structure in a community group. In: R. D. Hinshelwood & N. Manning (Eds.), *Therapeutic Communities—Reflections and Progress*. London: Routledge & Kegan Paul.

Gustafson, J. P. (1976). The pseudo-mutual small group or institution. *Human Relations*, 29: 989–997.

Hinshelwood, R. D. (1987). *What Happens in Groups: Psychoanalysis, the Individual and the Community*. London: Free Association Books.

James, O. (1986). The role of the nurse/therapist relationship in the therapeutic community. In: R. Kennedy, A. Heymans, & L. Tischler (Eds.), *The Family as In-patient*. London: Free Association Books.

Jaques, E. (1960). Disturbances in the capacity to work. *The Journal of Psychoanalysis*, 41: 357–367.

Kennard, D. (1983). *An Introduction to Therapeutic Communities*. London: Routledge.

Larkin, P. (1974). *High Windows*. London: Faber.

Main, T. F. (1946). The hospital as a therapeutic institution. In: J. Johns (Ed.), *The Ailment and Other Psychoanalytic Essays*. London: Free Association Books, 1989.

Main, T. F. (1957). The ailment. In: J. Johns (Ed.), *The Ailment and Other Psychoanalytic Essays*. London: Free Association Books, 1989.

Main, T. F. (1975). Some dynamics of large groups. In: J. Johns (Ed.), *The Ailment and Other Psychoanalytic Essays*. London: Free Association Books, 1989.

Main, T, F. (1983). The concept of a therapeutic community. In: J. Johns (Ed.), *The Ailment and Other Psychoanalytic Essays*. London: Free Association Books, 1989.

Meinrath, M. R., & Roberts, J. (1982). On being a good enough staff member. *International Journal of Therapeutic Communities*, 3: 7–14.

Miller, E. J., & Gwynne, G. (1972). *A Life Apart*. London: Tavistock.

Ogden, T. H. (1991). An interview with Thomas Ogden. *Psychoanalytic Dialogues*, 1: 361–376.

Peplau, H. E. (1952). *Interpersonal Relations in Nursing*. New York: Putnam.

Peplau, H. E. (1994). Psychiatric mental health nursing. *Journal of Psychiatric Mental Health Nursing*, 1: 3–7.

Roberts, V. (1994). The self assigned impossible task. In: A. Obholzer & V. Roberts (Eds.), *The Unconscious at Work*. London: Routledge.

Segal, H. (1956). Depression in the schizophrenic. In: *The Work of Hannah Segal*. New York: Jason Aronson, 1981.

Twain, M. (1976). *The Unabridged Mark Twain*. Philadelphia, PA: Running Press.

Weddell, D. (1968). Change of approach. In: E. Barnes (Ed.), *Psychosocial Nursing*. London: Tavistock.

Wilson, A. (1986). An outline of work with families at the Cassel Hospital. In: R. Kennedy, A. Heymans, & L. Tischler (Eds.), *The Family as In-patient* (pp. 49–63). London: Free Association Books.

Winnicott, D. W. (1960). Parent–infant relationships. In: *The Maturational Processes and the Facilitating Environment: Studies in the Theory of Emotional Development*. London: Hogarth Press. [Reprinted: London: Karnac Books, 1990.]

Winnicott, D. W. (1970). *Playing and Reality*. London: Tavistock.

Winship, G. (1995). Nursing and psychoanalysis—uneasy alliances. *Psychoanalytic Psychotherapy*, 9 (3): 289–299.

INDEX